# A
# COUNTRYWOMAN'S
# NOTES

*The Drawing Room, Barnsley House*

# A
# COUNTRYWOMAN'S
# NOTES
## by
## Rosemary Verey

*Foreword by*
*II.R.H. The Prince of Wales*

FRANCES LINCOLN

*A Countrywoman's Notes*
*Copyright © Gryffon Publications 1989*
*All rights reserved*
*No part of this publication may be reproduced, stored*
*in a retrieval system or transmitted, in any form, or*
*by any means, electronic, mechanical, photocopying,*
*recording or otherwise without prior written*
*permission of the publishers*

*British Library Cataloguing in Publication Data*
*Verey, Rosemary*
  *A Countrywoman's Notes*
  *1. Gardening*
  *I. Title*
  *635*

ISBN *0-7112-0693-7*

*Set in 12pt Garamond*

*Printed and bound in England by BPCC Hazell Books*

*First published in* Country Life *magazine in monthly
contributions between 1979 and 1987
Selected and edited by Eileen Stamers-Smith
Limited edition of 260 copies printed and published
in 1989 by Gryffon Publications, Barnsley, Gloucestershire*

*This edition published in association with
Gryffon Publications by
Frances Lincoln Limited
Apollo Works, 5 Charlton Kings Road,
London NW5 2SB*

*First Frances Lincoln Edition: October 1991*

*1 3 5 7 9 8 6 4 2*

*This book is dedicated to all my Barnsley friends, neighbours over fifty years*

# ENGRAVINGS

*The Drawing Room, Barnsley House*
by HOWARD PHIPPS ........................ Frontispiece
*January* by GEORGE TUTE ..................... Page 12
*Swans* by CHRISTOPHER WORMELL ...... Page 24
*Sketching* by MIRIAM MACGREGOR ......... Page 35
*Dirt Gardener* by MIRIAM MACGREGOR ... Page 39
*Stone Waller* by MIRIAM MACGREGOR ...... Page 41
*April* by ANTHONY CHRISTMAS ........... Page 48
*Gloucester Cows* by SARAH VAN NIEKERK Page 52
*June* by YVONNE SKARGON .................. Page 63
*Flowers* by YVONNE SKARGON ............. Page 68
*July* by JONATHAN GIBBS .................... Page 70
*Sun* by JONATHAN GIBBS ..................... Page 79
*August* by NICHOLAS JOHNSON ............ Page 82
*Barefoot* by NICHOLAS JOHNSON ........... Page 87
*Hay Bales* by RAY HEDGER ..................... Page 92
*Hay Stack* by RAY HEDGER ..................... Page 95
*Spider's Web* by JONATHAN GIBBS ......... Page 102
*Winter Walk* by BETTY PENNELL .......... Page 106
*Snow Scene* by HOWARD PHIPPS ............. Page 117

7

# CONTENTS

FOREWORD............................................ Page 10
*by H.R.H. The Prince of Wales*

JANUARY.............................................. Page 13
*Patterns, man-made and natural; Neolithic flints; Footprints in the snow; A seedsman's cabinet; An old mushroom house; Light; William Turk's horse collar; Foxes and hens; The village post office; Old diaries*

FEBRUARY............................................ Page 23
*Garden ghosts and skeletons; Bibury swans; A shell grotto; A nut tunnel; A warm February day; Compost making; Winter sweet; Village life*

MARCH................................................ Page 34
*Candlemas Day; Norman Jewson; Church offertory box; American expression; Our dogs; Stone walls*

APRIL................................................. Page 43
*Signs of spring; The shepherd of Banbury; Middleton Place; Hedgerows in April*

MAY.................................................. Page 51
*Double Gloucester cheese; Yellow oil-seed rape; Bees in the roof; Favourite seasons; Moles; Elderflower cordial*

JUNE................................................. Page 59
*June medley; Mignonette; Hawthorn and other blossoms; Herons; Seeing; Weather, wet or fine; Country receipts*

8

JULY ........................................................ Page 71
*Heatwave; Roadside verges; Bees; Village greens; Closing the local railways; Old photographic plates; Picnics*

AUGUST ................................................... Page 80
*A flower show; Thunderbugs; Countryside colours; Our green woodpeckers; Holly; Respecting the countryside; Straw burning*

SEPTEMBER ............................................... Page 88
*Seeds; My favourite weeks; Straw bales; Good neighbours; Hedgehogs*

OCTOBER .................................................. Page 96
*The western wind; Hedgerows; The colour of stone; Harlow Carr Gardens; The behaviour of birds; Spiders' webs*

NOVEMBER ............................................... Page 103
*Apple storing; Leaf-mould; Keeping a diary; A Gertrude Jekyll border; Christmas decorations*

DECEMBER ............................................... Page 111
*Violets, a signature of love; Drilling patterns; Garden scents; The shortest days; Conservation*

9

# FOREWORD

Some April mornings, Rosemary Verey is happy to be woken by the sound of rain coming from the south-east and beating hard against her windows at five o'clock. She knows it is helping the sand to sink in and annihilate the moss on her lawn. Few but the great gardeners of our time would welcome such an interruption. Mrs Verey is one of these. But be not daunted: she makes gardening seem the easiest and most natural thing in the world and, above all, throughout her countrywoman's notes there rests an air of complete contentment. She talks of Herb Robert (that very nice weed), of June strawberries, roses and peas, of the melancholy of February and the thrill of Spring, the hell of ground elder and the heaven of her chicken run and manages to make you feel extremely un-guilty that you have not pruned your plum tree.

The garden at Barnsley House (which I love and you must visit) comes to life; so too does the straggling lime-stone village, whose street I feel I have often walked, whose church I have entered and whose ancient track leading westward towards Coln St. Aldwyns, "haunted by ghosts of the past and full of good things in the hedges", is familiar.

It is this feeling of familiarity, of settled stability, of memory and of home which is so strong. It is always there in every English village that has witnessed the passing of generations, but by describing the minutiae of her days over the seasons, the goings on of bees, the picking of evergreen oak for a church flower arrangement, Mrs Verey evokes its very essence.

November sees and has always seen the collecting and storing of apples at Barnsley; once by her own children and now by her grandchildren. Although the village school has closed, the old village hierarchy changed, and not everybody is related to everyone else as they used to be, the continuity is there and there will always be a child at Barnsley to put flowers on his grandfather's grave in the churchyard.

Mrs Verey much reveres the world of Ernest Gimson and Sidney Barnsley, those dedicated Arts and Crafts practitioners from nearby Sapperton. They would have approved so much of these wonderful wood engravings whose depth is such a good medium for revealing the intricacies of hedgerows. And wouldn't William Morris have approved from across the willowy meadows in Kelmscott? After a beautiful house, the next thing to be longed for he said was "a Beautiful Book". Here is one.

_Charles_

# JANUARY

I enjoy patterns, man-made and natural, and as soon as I start looking around me, they are everywhere. The countryside in winter has tree skeletons silhouetted against the sky — trees without leaves. One day their background is dark grey, another it is clear blue, but there is always a natural pattern of trunk and branches, a lesson in symmetry with variations. As the snow slowly melts, man-made patterns, still filled with snow, scar the fields where the wheelmarks of tractors crossed the newly sown corn last autumn, sometimes straight, sometimes following the line of the walls or hedgerows. Then, looking up, you see a thin white line of snow clinging, still frozen, to the telegraph wires and television aerials. The snow on the tops of walls lasts much longer than on the soil all around. Look across the countryside and you will find a pattern created by the wall-builders years ago, a random pattern you may think, but as they worked the wall was dictated by the lie of the land, the farmer's whims and needful boundaries. The sheep have made their mark too — regular paths that they have walked crossing the hills for generations. We know man takes great pleasure in creating a sense of order by devising geometric shapes in architecture and gardens but when we see regularity in the world of nature we react with surprise. Snowflakes through the microscope, or fairy rings – have they happened by accident any more than the concentric circles on the pond when we throw in a stone and disturb its calm? Sounds have their pattern too. The repeated rhythmic song of the blackbird, the soft lilt of the woodpigeon, the cuckoo calling – these are more noticeable to our ears than the disorganised twitter of the house sparrows. Wherever you look or listen there is some pattern to discover, creating rhythm or calm satisfaction.

❋ ❋ ❋        ❋ ❋ ❋        ❋ ❋ ❋

Flints are not indigenous to our local countryside – the nearest source is the Marlborough Downs – so when you catch sight of worked flints as you walk across a newly ploughed field it naturally raises questions in your mind. Paleolithic implements are found in gravel and clay beds but the later Neolithic flints lie on or near the surface so ploughing turns them up. The flint is weathered and the black surfaces have, through age, become irregularly whitened with a dull lustre and with the edges slightly blunted but not water-worn. It is exciting to me to hold one of these in my hand and to realise that it could have been worked 5,000 years ago. The implements Neolithic man used and that we now find on the high ground of the Cotswolds are scrapers, arrowheads, stone hammers, flint flakes with serrated edges, burins and the remaining cores, lumps of flint left over. Where these flints are found there may have been continuous habitation for thousands of years, for pieces of Roman tile have also surfaced and I have found the shell of a Roman snail. When you are standing almost on the top of the Cotswolds, with only cattle and one farmhouse in view, it is comforting to feel that an unbroken chain of men have enjoyed it too. It gives strength to one's belief in eternity.

\* \* \*     \* \* \*     \* \* \*

What sacrilege it always seems to walk across the un-blemished smooth snow-covered land. It will never be the same again. Immediately round the house animals and birds have dared to come, early, before we are about. Is it the snow that has brought them or do they always haunt our garden, leaving no footprints behind? Michael, who lives just a mile out of our village, told me that the tracks of three deer came within 15 feet of his house. The deer live contentedly inside the park wall through most of the year but will venture out in search of food when hungry. Luckily sufficient snow prevented untoward damage in his garden. There were hare footmarks round our vege-table patch. Amusingly, probably only two of them had eaten every leaf of parsley standing above snow level. I am sure it did them good and if it had been left it would have been frosted by now. Every berry on the hollies and sorbus has been stripped. I do not grudge this, as I know the berries help the birds through difficult days. It is the berries left lying on the ground which annoy me. We have a beautiful pheasant and his mate living in the garden. Their activities, judging from tell-tale footprints, have been tremendous. However, they keep their distance from the house and confine their appearance to moments when humans are indoors. This is quite unlike a kestrel, which my family saw swooping down on the birds feeding on crumbs immediately outside their front door when they themselves were only a few yards away. It is also unlike the robin, who is so anxiously awaiting his crumbs to be put on the birdtable outside the kitchen door that he will peer in the kitchen window if I am not on time with his food.

     🙠 🙠 🙠     🙠 🙠 🙠     🙠 🙠 🙠

Some time ago I was invited to an antique shop to see a large wooden cabinet about to be shipped abroad. It rose from floor to ceiling and as far as I remember was at least 12 feet long. It was composed of a multitude of carefully graded drawers, each with a name on it; it was a seedsman's cabinet. The drawers pulled out smoothly and their size was obviously relative to the demand for a particular seed. There were flower seed names at one end, vegetables at the other, and four large drawers at the base announced peas and beans. It was similar in purpose to a modern filing-cabinet, or, more romantically, to an old set of chemist's drug-containers. Seed merchants are less numerous than chemists and I imagine their cabinets to be rarer. I found another of these cabinets, not in an antique shop but in the potting shed-cum-management area of a late Victorian walled kitchen garden. The drawers were empty but there it stood in lovely condition, waiting to be used once more. It was interesting to see the number of drawers allotted to each vegetable. There was plenty of space for peas and beans, only a small drawer for herbs, two each for carrots and parsnips, several for brassicas and lettuce and one small drawer for annuals. In this same garden I found something else I had not seen before—a special mushroom house. It has no windows, is built of brick, about 15 feet by 9 feet and high enough to accommodate three layers of 'bunks' on each side of a central passage. The bunks are brick-constructed and each layer is subdivided, presumably so that a constant rotation of mushroom cropping could be kept up. Closing my eyes I imagined the warmth that would have been generated by the decaying horse-manure collected from stables conveniently nearby and then prepared to exactly the right texture and temperature, the whole operation carefully overseen by one of those paragon head gardeners of large estates. With the complex task of growing enough flowers for the house, quantities of vegetables for the dining room and servants' hall, and thousands of bedding plants, they must have been talented men, not to mention green-fingered. They held secrets that no amount of technology can emulate.

\* \* \*     \* \* \*     \* \* \*

Some people are far more sensitive to light than others

17

and are at their happiest when there is plenty of sunlight and they can throw open the windows and walk outside. None of us is immune to seasonal changes, though we may think we are, but we are certainly less so than plants and animals. Fading and increasing light tells them to hibernate or drop their leaves, mate or be active. I welcome winter as a time when I can slightly change my way of life, stay indoors more, read, and give way to a lethargy I do not have in summer. I am aware that the light as it meets our eyes produces a set of nerve impulses that travel to the gland between the hemispheres of our brain, and that the hormones in this gland have a powerful effect on our sleep as well as our mood, so perhaps my lethargy is quite natural. "A sad tale's best for winter", wrote Shakespeare. I believe he meant this to fit the winter mood of the reader. I have just talked to a friend who is moving back to London after two winters and a summer in the country. She says she feels depressed in the country and wants the companionship and activity of town life. I am wondering if it is really the lack of sunlight through the naturally short days that she is missing rather than the glitter of town lights. Soon spring will be with us and the days much longer, so our spirits should be lightened too.

\* \* \*     \* \* \*     \* \* \*

In the days when villages had their own areas of common land, where all the inhabitants had equal rights to graze their animals, the question of ownership must have caused problems, and rustling of cattle and horses was surely a difficulty which had to be dealt with. In our village a farmer named William Turk took no risks with his horses, as we discovered recently when his horse collar came into our possession. It is made of a thin strip of steel about ½ inch broad, oval in shape with a hinge at one end and an elaborate locking system at the other. It fits exactly round the top of a horse's neck, large enough not to cause discomfort or chafing but small enough to make it impossible to remove except with its two-ended key. On a brass inlay round the collar is the inscription in clear 18th century calligraphy: "Stolen from Wm. Turk, Barnsley, Glorshire". Both father and son Turk are buried in the churchyard. The horse collar was made by a Birmingham firm called Hiatt, which has been established for over 200 years and still makes handcuffs.

*　*　*　　　*　*　*　　　*　*　*

Foxes get hungry just now and given half a chance will take precious young pullets and tough old hens. Wonderful words of country wisdom come easily from Mrs Hart as she and I do the washing up together. Her hens, kept in a large wire-enclosed run, lay well, and neither she nor they have a sleepless night when foxes are visiting the neighbouring poultry. The small door into the hen-house is never closed but the doorway has a couple of iron chains hanging down over the entrance. When the ground has been snow-covered, a fox's footmarks have reached the chains, then turned away. Could it be an instinctive fear that the chains are a trap? I like to hear from Mrs Hart about the postman who used to bicycle four miles to our village each morning, made his delivery, then brewed tea and waited in a tiny cottage (just one up and one down) until afternoon to allow the villagers time to answer their mail. He sold them stamps and bicycled back into town punctually for the letters to be sorted and arrive at their destinations the next morning; and this for the price of 1d. But that was before my day. When I came here we had our own post office where Mrs Messenger sold stamps and sweets in the front room and second-hand clothes in the back. She was well patronised as those were the days of clothes coupons. Later Mrs Turner had the post office and it was the hub of village life. You could buy all sorts of things, from Reckitt's blue and hairnets to chocolate bars and tinned dog food; with time to spare you could pick up the village gossip too. Incidentally the Reckitt's blue was not, as you would expect, for the wash tubs, but was kept specially for the owner of the Shire stallion to rinse his great horse's white feathers in before going to a show. Now we just have a letter box with no means of acquiring stamps, local news or anything else.

✍ ✍ ✍          ✍ ✍ ✍          ✍ ✍ ✍

This is the kind of weather when we need a good book and a good fire. My thoughts, not surprisingly considering the below zero temperature, are centred round what it is like outside, so I have turned to some famous old diaries. From 1768 until 1793, Gilbert White kept the most published natural history diary the world has ever known. It is a lovely book, conjuring up in one's mind the other seasons, when "young partridges and pheasants abound" and "vast crops of plums, currants and gooseberries". Today our wind is coming from Russia, causing the light and flaky snow to drift, travelling parallel with the top of my garden wall, dancing reels across the lawn. On this same day in 1776, Gilbert White's entry reads: "Rugged Siberian weather. The narrow lanes are full of snow in some places which is driven into most romantic and grotesque shapes. The road wagons are obliged to stop and the stage coaches are much embarrassed. I was obliged to be much abroad on this day and scarce ever saw its fellow." I wonder how they managed. Birds were suffering in mid-January 1775: "Mr. H.'s man says that he caught in a lane near Hackwood many rooks which attempting to fly fell from the trees with their wings frozen together by the sleet that froze as it fell. There were, he affirms, many dozens so disabled." In the following century the Rev. Francis Kilvert, too, had interesting things to say, though they tended to be more about the lovely country girls than the weather. In 1871 he wrote: "A soft sunny showery morning and it felt like spring as we walked to Claremont soon after noon." In 1872 it was evidently even warmer, for he wrote: "The air early this morning was as warm as the air of a hot-house and the thrushes singing like mad

21

thinking the spring has come." In contrast, his mid-January entry for 1779 reads: "Last night the river rose rapidly and at midnight the ice was rushing down in vast masses, roaring, cracking and thundering against the bridge like the rolling of a hundred wagons. By morning the river had sunk and left huge piles of ice stranded on the banks."

# FEBRUARY

It is not only sunny days that make for memorable and sometimes unexpected sights when the eye is taken by surprise. "Exclusiveness in a garden is a mistake as great as it is in society," wrote Alfred Austin, author of *The Garden that I love*. How I would have enjoyed a conversation with him one morning as I walked round the garden looking for special situations due to the freezing fog which enveloped me and most of the surrounding plants. Best of all was Miss Willmott's Ghost *(Eryngium giganteum)* or rather the skeleton of her ghost (can a ghost have a skeleton?) looking ravishing with the edges of her remains rimmed with frozen fog – how fortunate that she had not been cut down and consigned to the bonfire in the autumn. So absorbed did I become in my thoughts of skeletons and ghosts and hoping that Alfred Austin was enjoying himself that I almost expected Miss Ellen Willmott to glide through the mist and join our conversation. As I walked on there were more exciting skeletons, a solitary spike of *Ligularia clivorum*, left there to spread its seeds, and several brown stems of the herbaceous *Phlomis samia* which I like to keep for the tits to swing on as they feed on the seeds. The tall remains of *Crambe cordifolia* were there to remind me of summer in this foggy, frosty day when every leaf was edged white

with ice. The white rims of frozen fog round the ever-green berberis looked like the white edge on the wings of a large blue butterfly. It made me wonder what exactly white is, and I discovered that it is sometimes caused by physical effects. It can be due to air spaces within tissues where the reflection of light makes an impression of white-ness. The white or grey of *Senecio* White Diamond is the reflection from the innumerable hairs which cover the leaves, with air between each. Snow and frost, made up of colourless ice crystals with air spaces, have the same effect—whiteness. A solid block of ice is colourless but ice full of air bubbles becomes white.

❖ ❖ ❖        ❖ ❖ ❖        ❖ ❖ ❖

A pair of swans have nested here for years and raised successive families. These birds are long-lived and once they pair they are usually faithful to their mate for life, so there was considerable consternation in Bibury when, taking off from her nest at the Trout Farm, the pen flew into a passing lorry and was killed. The cob was lonely and desolate but at least the seven cygnets were old enough to fend for themselves and later dispersed down the river to find new territory. Another disaster had occurred three miles away at Coln St. Aldwyns when a cob swan flew into overhead electric cables and was killed, leaving his mate alone. Now, much to the satisfaction of the Bibury inhabitants, their cob and the pen from Coln have got together. We will be waiting anxiously to discover whether or not the new pen is mature enough to raise a family this year.

✤ ✤ ✤          ✤ ✤ ✤          ✤ ✤ ✤

One might imagine there could be little enjoyment in garden visiting on a chilly February Sunday, but quite the contrary. We were lunching near Bristol and our host was amazed to discover that I had never seen the famous shell grotto at Goldney House, Clifton. A wealthy Bristol merchant, Thomas Goldney, began building it in 1737, taking 27 years to complete it. The work of covering the walls with shells and fossils not only occupied hours, but collecting these amazingly beautiful objects no doubt took years to achieve. The approach from the house is dramatic, through an avenue of tall yews, their trunks bare to 20 feet or more, gleaming red in the late afternoon sun. As you get nearer you are aware that the land falls sharply down beyond and below the garden, so when you descend the steps and open the grotto door, it is a panorama of Bristol and the river Avon you expect. Instead you find yourself in a haunting but beautiful cavern, the roof supported by four pillars, encrusted, as are the walls, with precious jewel-like shells, great bowls of mother-of-pearl, fossilised coral and ammonites, small sea shells and huge conch shells in which you can hear the sea roaring. A marble Neptune reclines with his trident at the top of a narrow cleft, water tumbles from an urn into a shallow pool. Guarding the treasures are a lion and lioness in their den. Inside this subterranean hall we sheltered from the wind on a cold winter's day, but how cool and refreshing it would be in high summer. Other pleasures await the visitor in this garden, not least the exciting view from the top of the tower above the grotto. The leafless trees allowed us a full panorama through their branches. Goldney House now belongs to Bristol University and is open on certain days in the summer.

* * *         * * *         * * *

Philip Miller, gardener to the Worshipful Company of Apothecaries at their Botanic Garden at Chelsea, wrote in 1732 that December was the darkest month of the whole year. Adding up the hours of darkness I am sure he must be right but for me February is the most dreary month. We are almost at the end of the tunnel and perhaps it is the accumulation of dark days that do their best to get me down. Luckily they do not succeed as there is wonderful promise of things to come. Yesterday as I drove down 'Welsh Way', a 2000 year old lane near our village, I got out of my car to examine the nut trees. They grow each side of the lane making a wonderful canopy, joining hands in the middle. At night, with car headlights full on, you feel as though you are driving through a magic tunnel. We all know the golden tassels of the male flowers covered with pollen, but less conspicuous are the clusters of small red female blossoms, now open and ready to receive pollen from the catkins. They are small but you may see the

27

bunch of bright crimson pistils enclosed within green bracts. When they are fertilised an odd thing happens, unique I believe in our garden happenings. The flower is growing on last year's wood but as soon as it is fertilised it starts away from the old wood and forms behind itself a thin twig, four or five inches long, at the end of which it ripens into a nut. As it travels it carries with it the bract in which the flower was formed and this becomes the cup in which the nut will lie. The leafy cup has given its name to the tree: *Corylus*, from the Greek meaning a cap or helmet. It is native to Britain and the old British name was *Haesel—haesle* is a cap or hat and the *haesel-nutu* is the hatted nut. Whatever the weather, there will always be some phenomenon of nature to pause beside and admire, to learn from and tuck into one's memory.

ย ย ย        ย ย ย        ย ย ย

At breakfast time the sun came pouring through the kitchen window, luring me outside. I opened the cold frames so that the hundreds of rooted cuttings would get the full benefit of the sunshine and then wandered through the garden. Not only did everything look much better than on the previous gloomy day but there was unmistakably a scene of spring around the corner. I turned back to put the maximum/minimum thermometer on the stone table—a bit of a cheat perhaps as it is our warmest corner with the sun reflecting back from lichen-covered stone. The thermometer rose to 60 degrees F. I could hardly

28

believe my own ears when I heard the bees working. I have been worrying so much about them; could they possibly survive the ordeal of our below-zero temperatures? There they were, at least ten of them, industriously collecting pollen from a small group of snowdrops, *Galanthus elwesii*, with their wide leaves and long outer petals, the inner petals with splunges of green in a pattern reminiscent of the bees' yellow markings. They were intensely busy and obviously delighted to be out on their earliest forage of the year. I hurried on and found more bees on the suddenly wide-open aconite flowers and pollen-laden willows. That Sunday evening I found my explanation of the bees' resistance to extreme cold in Maurice Maeterlinck's *The Life of the Bee*, first published in English in 1901 (our copy is 1912). Row upon row of bees, with the queen in their midst, cling to the combs from whose honey they slowly feed in the winter. When the outer bees feel the cold stealing over them they re-enter the mass and others take their outside places. The author continues: "By the concerted beating of their wings, which go quickly or slowly in accordance as the temperature outside may vary, they maintain in their sphere an unchanging warmth, equal to that of a day in spring."

❋ ❋ ❋          ❋ ❋ ❋          ❋ ❋ ❋

Our chicken-run with its twelve hens and handsome cock must be as productive as any; I do not mean for eggs but for the wonderfully rich compost the hens make for us. The idea came to me after reading about compost-making in the Royal Horticultural Society's Journal, *The Garden*, in 1976. It was a scientific article about composi-tions of organic matter, temperature/time patterns and nutrients. I could not understand it until the penultimate page where there was a photograph of an old wooden chest and an equally old-fashioned chicken-run. I read: "Compost production can be integrated with small free-range poultry-keeping to good effect. Wastes can be stored in the run where the hens will fragment, mix and fertilise them." Ever since that day all our garden weeds (except the wicked ones like ground elder), kitchen waste, lawn mowings, dying leaves from the Brussels sprouts, get thrown into the run. The hens love it and immediately they see the wheelbarrow about 20 yards away they start queueing at the gate in anticipation of goodies. I must say that they thrive on their fare, which apart from the garden waste consists only of a daily handful of corn each. In wet weather and when the supply from the garden is minimal, a bale of straw is scattered in their run. The build-up is rapid and the rot-down dramatic, aided by the free nitrogen from the hens' droppings. The next event is to remove the material from the run. Here I am fortunate as my farmer son comes twice a year—in spring and autumn—and with tractor and fork-lift the job is soon done. He skims the top foot or so and this forms the base of a new heap. By the time the final layer comes out the result is a good friable loam which is ready to use on the borders or as a base for our potting compost. We test this from time to time and have never found a major deficiency.

ɔ ɔ ɔ      ɔ ɔ ɔ      ɔ ɔ ɔ

One day 27 years ago, long before I became an enthusiastic gardener, my husband came home with a bush of winter sweet, given to him by an old lady from her garden. She said it would not flower for seven years and then for ever after would do so generously. She was right. I always appreciate its wonderful scent and bring small sprigs indoors on Christmas day and all through January. Slowly it has been growing over one of our drawing-room windows, which it now completely covers. The decision has been made; it must be pruned down to window-sill level. So I have been cutting long luxurious branches covered in buds and open flowers and we have revelled in the fragrance of the rather sinister waxy yellow and red flowers. Will it flower next year after such drastic pruning? Only time will tell and I hope that the kind old lady, now dead, will intercede for us and it.

\* \* \*      \* \* \*      \* \* \*

Village life, like human character, never stands still; it either improves or gets worse but the influences at work are beyond the control of the inhabitants. The motor car, a television set in every home and the demand for better living conditions, are some of the most important. Modern mechanisation means fewer farm workers and simple economics dictate the employment of fewer grooms and gardeners. In our village, cottages difficult to modernise without high cost have been sold and better homes have been built for the reduced number of employees. The population has changed, for better or worse; I strongly believe the former. The trend is for the erstwhile farm cottages to be enlarged and given all mod. cons. by their owner-occupiers, our new country-dwellers who commute each day by car to work in neighbouring towns. Some 20 years ago there were village theatricals and dances in the winter, Lent reading evenings in spring, and the high spot of midsummer was the fête, with bowling for the pig (always a present from our generous local farmer) and a great deal of talent-spotting. Some organised, others followed, but all joined in. Then gradually the television took over and we became watchers instead of doers. Village life took a downward turn; the Women's Institute and Rifle Club faded, dances dwindled, and when our postmistress died no one was public-spirited enough to take on her job. Worst of all, as there were (temporarily, as it proved) only a tiny handful of children under 11, our village school was closed. The Thrift Club and the Village Hall Committee are two bright spots which have carried on. Now suddenly our village is coming to life once more. There was a flutter of revival in Jubilee Year and with our newcomers full of initiative and enthusiasm a community feeling is positively returning. Previously this feeling depended on village hierarchy; now I believe it will rely far more on local talent and the will to be involved without a prod from the squire. We are coming full circle but there are subtle differences. Formerly, everyone knew each other, for they either worked together or were related; now they will have to become friends through their local leisure activities — the village fête this summer, or the weekly keep-fit class. Last Christmas over 30 children enjoyed a party in the church hall, which had not happened since the school was closed. Next we may have a Sunday School, and even a team of bellringers.

# MARCH

Candlemas Day came in "fair and bright" and winter certainly "had another flight". So the old saying was proved right. I am pleasantly surprised how many people have mentioned this to me in the past few days. Here we had two weeks of hard frost in February, which proved to be the exact treatment needed to control the over-precocious bulbs showing an unwonted amount of growth. However, I was anxious lest the aconites and dwarf iris, already in flower, should succumb. On the contrary, everything has behaved magnificently. The aconites have never looked so good for so long, from mid-January until the end of February; the iris have spanned the frosty days, and all the early crocus were held back until the sun came out and the temperature rose enough to entice the bees from their hives.

❖ ❖ ❖        ❖ ❖ ❖        ❖ ❖ ❖

In August 1907 Norman Jewson, a young, newly-qualified architect, stepped out of the train at Cirencester station. It was the turning point of his life when he arrived in "the capital of the Cotswolds", as he called this country market town. Jewson then chose what would seem to us a novel way of travel: he hired a donkey and trap from a nearby farmer and carried his camping equipment with

him. These were peaceful and satisfactory days for him,
for he fell in love with the Cotswold countryside and stone-
built villages, scenes that provided him with wonderful
material for his sketchbook. On his second evening, he
and the donkey having climbed a steep hill, he saw, silhouetted against the skyline, a man ploughing with two
yokes of oxen—an unusual sight even in those days. He
spent a month in the north Cotswolds, discovering and
sketching churches and old manor houses. In one village
he came on a group of almshouses being built by Edwin
Lutyens. All these sights excited and inspired the young
architect and the culmination of his journey was his meeting with Ernest Gimson, the Arts and Crafts architect and
furniture designer then living and working in Sapperton.
Here in the Cotswolds Gimson had found a perfect place
to live out his idealistic lifestyle and carry on his work. A
chord was struck between the two men and Jewson

immediately decided to move to Sapperton and work under Gimson, which he did until the latter's death in 1919. Norman Jewson's work has a dignity and simplicity in keeping with the traditional Cotswold manner. Under Gimson's guidance he learnt to do plasterwork, and many of his houses are decorated with his charming animal and floral patterns. He paid great attention to detail, with work such as wooden door-latches, carved newel-posts, decorative date-stones and beautifully cast lead work. All these characteristic details give his work a feeling of fine craftsmanship. He was a most modest man and perhaps overshadowed by his brilliant colleagues—Gimson himself, Ernest Barnsley the architect, Sidney Barnsley the designer and furniture-maker, and the talented cabinet-maker Peter Waals. At the time the work of all these great craftsmen received insufficient recognition, but today Gimson's and the Barnsleys' work is honoured and admired, and Jewson's autobiography of his early years spent working with Gimson, *By Chance I did Rove*, has been republished by Gryffon Publications, Barnsley, Gloucestershire.

\* \* \*  \* \* \*  \* \* \*

I recently discovered that the wall money-box in our church was overflowing—there was no room for another penny. The problem was how to open it. I went to ask the advice of our wonderful and now retired treasurer, who has kept the church accounts for at least forty years and is now only just short of 100. No problem, he told me, all I would need was an old tin-opener. Armed with a reasonably old one I went to the church but had no immediate success and put the whole issue out of my mind. In the meantime friends had started searching for an old Chubb key to do the trick. It had become quite a challenge. Things often turn up in unexpected places, and as I was searching for something quite different I came on a box-file with a sticker saying "Barnsley P.C.C." in the treasurer's handwriting. Nervously I opened it and was rewarded with two excitements. First a £5 premium bond lay on top. It was issued in January 1955 so our church should be due for a windfall any time now. Better still, here was the old tin-opener. It must have been the very one that was used to open the wall money-box, for tied to it was a piece of faded red ribbon and attached to that was the missing Chubb key. It all seemed too good to be true and the treasurer had been right about the importance of the old-style tin-opener.

\* \* \*    \* \* \*    \* \* \*

I was delighted to read in "Letter from Tokyo" in *The Times* that we are not the only nation to regard dogs as of importance in our lives. I quote: "Dogs in Japan have never had it so good since the late seventeenth century when a law was passed that all dogs must be treated kindly and addressed only in the most polite terms." It is a common axiom in England that sooner or later owners grow like their dogs; or is it that instinctively they choose

37

the dog which is most like them in the first place? My country neighbours have well-mannered shooting dogs, sometimes smooth-coated labradors or exuberant spaniels, friendly and long-eared. Apart from the ears they become very alike. The shepherd and cowman have their obedient collies with their quick movements and alert habit, friendly and decisive. Then there are the ladies with their whippets or dachshunds, smart, neat and reasonably well-behaved. One sees few Yorkshire or Skye terriers these days. It was my ambition as a child to have a Skye terrier, influenced by a favourite book, but instead I was given a Sealyham called Kim. However much I groomed him, he never looked sleek. I also had the care of my brother's bull terrier while he was abroad. This I enjoyed, especially taking him on exercise through the lanes on my bicycle. He was rather ugly, much too bouncy and rather a way-ward character. Then came a wonderful rough-haired dachshund, intelligent, sporting, great fun as a friend and surprisingly adept at catching rabbits. He was a bit of a Londoner, too, enjoying weaving through the traffic or jumping on buses. I wonder now which of the character-istics of those three dogs rubbed off on me as a teenager? Take a walk through any park or common land where dogs are exercised and sure enough there will be the strong young man with his Doberman, all powerful shoulders and controlled aggression. Is he an expression of his master's ego? And the lady in her sixties, rather hunched and limping but jolly—look round and you will find her canine companion is a jaunty Pekingese or a friendly terrier. One thing is certain, sooner or later the dog-owners will get talking to each other and barriers will be broken, and all because of the dogs.

꙳ ꙳ ꙳          ꙳ ꙳ ꙳          ꙳ ꙳ ꙳

Americans speak English but often their expressions are far removed from ours. On one occasion I was introduced as a "dirt gardener". I felt mildly surprised and even embarrassed—did my fingernails so easily betray my daily occupation? Later I learnt it was intended as a compliment, to convey that I actually dig in the garden myself. A shared appreciation of a subject or a mutual way of life is the best way to seal a friendship.

Stonewalling is one of those country crafts which to the uninitiated townsman may seem simple. But stand and watch a skilled stonewaller at work and you will soon think differently. From a pile of stones beside him he will quickly select that of precisely the correct shape, size and thickness, sometimes knocking off an awkward corner, always laying it at an angle to discourage driving rain and snow from seeping inwards, and always keeping the sides of the wall unerringly straight. I have recently been watching the building of a five-foot high wall between a new garden and a paddock. It is made of old and new stones, the two intermingled, the old with their darkened texture, the newly-quarried standing out visually with their pale, almost raw, appearance. I like the chequered look. It reminds me that, however much machines and computers will eventually do for us, the creative art of stonewalling will always need a man's skill. In a year or two the new stones will have mellowed and grown lichens just as our garden wall has done. Our wall was built in 1770 so it has had time to become weathered. Coming home to look at it with a critical eye, I realised that it, too, has its own chequered look where an almost white lichen has grown in ever-widening circles on certain stones. How fast do lichens grow? Several years ago Oleg Polunin suggested I should take photographs to record their progress. I wish I had done so; there would be a positive answer by now. Another neighbour was altering the layout of her stable-yard, and in doing so a portion of wall was pulled down.

Inside, among the rubble filling the cavity between the two sides, Colin, who was doing the work, found a Wills cigarette carton, dated 1885. It was in perfect condition and when he opened it he discovered a screw of tinfoil with cigarette ash. What was remarkable was the absolute dryness of the carton, a sign of the skill with which the wall was built, to make sure every drop of water drained outwards at once. This is the secret, I am told, of a wall's long life. The initial cost of wall-building is astronomical, compared with that of making a wooden fence or planting a hedge, but in these latter cases the after-care has to be taken into account. When nearby road-widening was done a few years ago, the owner's choice was a stock-proof fence with a hawthorn hedge planted on its road side. I have been watching this hedge grow up and last autumn was delighted to notice that the time had come to cut and lay it. It looks beautiful now and will soon be solid enough to keep in any stock. But the cost of maintenance goes on, whereas a wall is a long-term investment.

# APRIL

Spring means the warming up of the soil. The appearance of the first flush of annual weeds is better than any thermometer to put you wise over this, telling you that you can start to sow your seeds outside with a sure conviction that they will germinate. On some spring days I imagine I can see the plants growing, especially when the earth smells good. This morning as I went outside in the sunshine after rain, the familiar smell of the balsam poplars wafted my way. The delicious resinous scent is strongest as the leaf buds are opening in April. Another sure sign of spring, and almost merging into summer, is the arrival of the swallows. As soon as they come we must remember to leave a crack in the garage doors to allow them inside. They always build in the rafters above the windscreen of my car. The poets have got it right. Chaucer chose "Aprille with his schowres swoote" as the pleasantest month for his Canterbury pilgrims to "go on pilgrimage". Spenser describes it as

> Garnished with garlands goodly dight
> Of all the fairest flowers and freshest buds
> Which the earth brings forth.

I particularly like John Evelyn's spring advice to his gardener at Sayes Court in 1687: "Never expose your

Oranges, Limons, and the like tender Trees whatever seasons flatter, 'til the Mulberry puts forth its leafe, then bring them boldly out of the Green House." Presumably the mulberry waits to put forth its leaf until all danger of frost is over, so the advice should hold good for one's geraniums and other tender bedding plants.

№ № №          № № №          № № №

The air was still and the weatherman had informed us that there would be rain before evening, so we decided it was a good day for spreading the lawn sand — an expensive gesture to keep on top of the ever-thriving moss on our lawn. For the lawn sand to do its job efficiently, it must rain within 48 hours, and as it had rained at some point during every 24 hours in the past month we thought we were not being unduly optimistic. When evening came, every black cloud passed us by, denying us that rain we so badly wanted. Next morning was clear and bright but we were cheered by the forecast: rain. By evening it was still dry, so, hoping for a wisp of consolation, I turned to *The Shepherd of Banbury's Rules to Judge the Changes of the Weather*. These I had recently found in *The Complete Weather Guide* of 1812. Who the shepherd of Banbury was is not stated but his rules were first published in 1744 by Mr Claridge. The latter declares that, to someone like the shepherd, with his 40 years of experience, the sun, wind, moon, stars, clouds, flowers and almost every animal were instruments of knowledge. I felt I could put my

44

trust in him. The evening sky was red, at first glance a sure sign of a fine day ahead. But the rain signs were about as well; small clouds were increasing; there were clouds at the top of the hills, "clouds at a great height striped like feathers in the breast of a hawk". It was all there, prognosticating rain. I went to bed happy, and sure enough, by 5 a.m. the rain woke me, coming from the south-east and beating hard against my windows. The lawn sand was being soaked into the ground and working to annihilate the moss. I picked up the weather book from my bedside, in gratitude to the shepherd of Banbury and hoping for more reassurance, but was not altogether pleased with what I read. "The difference between rising at five and at seven o' clock in the morning, for the space of forty years, is nearly equivalent to the addition of ten years to a man's life." Suppose you do not get up until 8 a.m. I wondered; but it was too difficult, my calculator was downstairs.

＊ ＊ ＊        ＊ ＊ ＊        ＊ ＊ ＊

The Anglican church we went to one recent Sunday in Charleston, South Carolina, was packed to overflowing with people squashed into square Georgian box pews. After the service our hosts Charles and Carol Duell and their four children showed us round their beautiful 18th century town house, which in the afternoon would be crowded with sightseers. Their plantation, Middleton Place, is 15 miles outside the town; the original house built 200 years ago was burnt down in the Civil War. The plantation has prospered during these two centuries on successful rice, cotton and indigo crops, replaced now by tourists, so we were not surprised to hear from Charles that he is shortly to speak at a conference on the subject of successful maintenance of historic estates. A carriage and pair takes visitors from the car park round the sweeping drive towards the house and plantation buildings. Here the blacksmith and carpenter are at work, pottery is being made, spinning and weaving goes on using home-produced wool, and the old homing mill is grinding corn. Old tools are on display and so are carriages and harness. The garden is a happy mixture, for in 1741 when Henry Middleton began its design he had recently returned from Europe and was strongly influenced by Le Nôtre. He devised a central axis looking towards the Ashley River, on one side of which he created precise patterns of formal symmetry. Much became overgrown and the design was almost lost over the years, but now it is once again revealed and restored to its original intent with box-edged beds and sunken gardens, a mount, a sundial and an octagon garden. These are surrounded by hundreds of indigenous live oaks dramatically festooned with Spanish moss; one oak is estimated to be over 1,000 years old. The woodland has been underplanted with camellias, the earliest dating from 1786 when the Frenchman Michaux visited Middleton; and there is an abundance of azaleas, magnolias, dogwoods and wisteria. A century-old *Osmanthus fragrans* is 25 feet tall and flowers profusely. Previously it was only the celebrated grass terraces and 'butterfly' lakes which were familiar to me from photographs.

After lunch we hurried off to a meet of the Middleton Place drag hounds. The season proper had finished, but a dozen stalwarts, including our host, who is Master, set off dressed in ratcatchers and leathers. Hounds soon picked up the line and we watched the field take on obstacles and away. Non-jumping followers are called 'hill-toppers'. In a quick word with the huntsman I discovered that he had a hound from England, the Duke of Beaufort's 'Democrat', some of whose progeny were hunting that day. This made me feel at home.

*℮ ℮ ℮*      *℮ ℮ ℮*      *℮ ℮ ℮*

In early April, especially this cold spring, the hedge-rows look misleadingly lifeless, the skeletons of the trees and bushes still without leaves. But much is happening or has happened already. Rabbits scurry along the hedges, and pheasants do the same, their colours merging into the pattern of the twigs. Hares with their March madness rely on their long legs to make a quick getaway across plough and grassland. Most self-respecting animals use the hedgerows as a highway from one destination to another. Hedgehogs are awake, hedge-sparrows are busy, the hedge-brown butterfly will not be about until later but you may see a small tortoiseshell, a peacock and even a brimstone. A lot of wild plants have 'hedge' in their

47

name and I am making a list of them for my grandson in the hope that he will find them all before the year is over. There is a Jack-run-along-the-hedge growing all up our lane, with starry white flowers and leaves that smell of garlic when you crush them. Gerard recommends using this for sauce with your fish. The sweet-smelling violets will be in flower by now and so will the hedge-violets, otherwise known as dog-violets, but these lack any scent. In Somerset, Herb Robert is known as Jack-by-the-hedge; I know it as Robin's eye, and its leaf has a strong, slightly unpleasant smell. In my hunting days, when we came home with a horse with a cut leg, we bound several leaves under the bandage and this had a wonderful healing effect. Pig-in-the-hedge is what they call blackthorn in Hampshire. I know that spring will not be here until after it has flowered. My Gloucestershire friends have a better name for it, heg-pegs, and they make use of the sloes later in the year. There are many other hedge-named plants; bindweed is called hedge-bells and ground ivy hedge-maids. Gerard knew *scutellaria* as hedge-hyssop but I like its other name, skull-cap, better—it is more descriptive. There is never any chance of missing goose grass; it will cling to you as its name, cleavers, indicates, but I have only just discovered that some people call it hedge-hogs.

❖ ❖ ❖        ❖ ❖ ❖        ❖ ❖ ❖

A regular end-of-April expedition we look forward

to going to see is the wild *Pulsatilla vulgaris*. There they are in their hundreds on a steep west-facing limestone bank, their blue heads hanging down. To get the best view of them you must walk across the hillside, always looking upward. The stems are only an inch or two long, which helps to camouflage the flowers. One year on our way home we suddenly saw a pair of hoopoes, presumably going to their summer breeding-ground. Their very distinctive crests make them easily recognisable. One quickly flew over the hedge into the adjoining field and the other kept immediately in front of our car for a matter of 100 yards or more as we drove slowly along; it was an afternoon to remember. The bank of pulsatillas is a site specially protected by the Gloucestershire Trust for Nature Conservation. Obviously the plants must not be dug up or picked and the owner of the farm has agreed to keep grazing animals off the site in early spring to allow enough time for the full development of the flowers and seed dispersal. The Trust does valuable work, with 50 nature reserves and a network of protected sites. It is also very active in the field of education, with projects for adults and to encourage schoolchildren to become interested in the world about them.

# MAY

I was so pleased to read about a farmhouse industry with a difference. At The Banks, Newent, in Gloucestershire, Mr John Crisp and his wife, realising that Double Gloucester cheese was made only in the surrounding counties, decided to rectify the situation. They started a farmhouse cheese-making dairy using traditional methods with milk from their own small herd of Gloucester cows. Now, years later, they have a thriving business thanks to their seven breeding Gloucesters and their own industry. Their products are sold locally and also by some London stores. Double Gloucester is a strong-tasting orange-coloured cheese, and the single is a milder, creamy light-coloured cheese. The farm is open to the public three times a week for people to watch the cheese making in progress. This takes from 8 a.m. until 4.30 p.m. and the cheese then needs four months to mature. Mrs Crisp has emphasised to me that as watching space is limited she appreciates it if intending visitors will ring beforehand. The Crisps' dream is to start up a working farm museum, incorporating cheese and butter making and showing local rare breeds of livestock. The farm is only thirty miles from my home but it was not until I was crossing the James River in Virginia that I heard about it. We were near the Berkeley Plantation and I asked in

a lighthearted way if it had got its name from Berkeley, Gloucestershire. Indeed, settlers had arrived there in 1618 from Gloucestershire, the heart of the cheese-making country. Not surprisingly, on the bills of lading on the small ships that carried the travellers there were considerable amounts of cheese—an excellent form of food that would keep well on the voyage. I read about this and the Newent cheese-making in an American publication sent out by the Association of Living History, Farms and Museums.

* * *     * * *     * * *

An amusing and interesting discussion arose yesterday when I asked a group of Americans from California what struck them most about our countryside. "Its greenness" was their immediate answer. The hedgerows and trees have changed now from brown to green. When you stop to consider, green is the predominant colour of our countryside and when huge fields of the strident yellow oil-seed rape make a sheet of bright colour, you wonder if you like it. I do. I know it is only momentary and it lightens the landscape from dawn to dusk, and even by moonlight. Counting these fields is an occupying game for children when they are making a long journey from one side of England to the other. Travelling between East Anglia and Gloucestershire, the wife of one of my farming neighbours said her children stopped counting when they reached 250. "Why does no one develop paler yellow or

53

even white rape flowers?" one American lady asked. We discussed how pretty the fields would look—just like an enormous spring garden planted with white honesty and yellow tulips.

*   *   *                  *   *   *                  *   *   *

The bees have given me a terrible fright this spring. They live in our roof and have done as long as I can remember. We rely on them for fertilising the fruit blossom and for many other services around the garden, including just being there to watch and enjoy. They make their first sortie on a sunny day in February to gather pollen from the willow catkins and wide-open crocuses, and from then on I see them around on sunny days. This year there was no sign of them, either working in the garden or going in and out of the roof. I value them so highly that I was beginning to make plans to get a hive ready for another swarm; but this would not have been quite the same; the roof-dwelling bees are old friends. I could hardly believe my eyes a few days later when I looked up and there, silhouetted against the sky, was a crowd of bees flying lazily around, going slowly in and out of the roof tiles as if they had only just woken. What could they have been doing these last three months? Obviously if I want to know I must go to an official source such as Hartpury, near Gloucester, where the County College of Horticulture includes bee-keeping on the curriculum. Meanwhile I have been discussing the problem with any sympathetic listener. An American visitor who is an official bee inspector told me that either the queen had died or else the whole colony had perished from a disease. Another suggestion was that mice in the roof had stolen the winter supply of honey and the bees had starved to death. I am quite accustomed at night to the sound of scurrying in the wainscoting and ceiling above my bed, and am never certain whether it is mice or starlings in the eaves, or perhaps a bit of both. The sounds recently have been noisy enough to be extra-fat mice feeding on honey. The real answer is likely to remain a mystery, as no self-respecting builder or bee-keeper will happily volunteer to take tiles off the roof to investigate, with the prospect of thousands of bees attacking him while he is on the top of a ladder 30 feet up.

❖ ❖ ❖      ❖ ❖ ❖      ❖ ❖ ❖

Spring is my favourite season of the year, at least I always think so when I see the leaf buds on the trees bursting dramatically into green. A similar feeling comes over me in October as the leaves take on their autumn colours. Both of these seasons have their individual charm; in spring it is the assurance that all will be lush, green and urgent for the next few months; autumn has a passing beauty and allows time to relax. It is impossible to decide which is best, but there is no need to; all that is necessary is to enjoy the present. Here in Gloucestershire, I gather we are behind counties such as Somerset, Kent and

Herefordshire, but this does not matter as we will catch up. While the garden is full of bright yellows and reds, many trees in the countryside are laden with their less conspicuous flowers. These are easy to overlook if you think they are the leaf buds opening. From my window I can see the 5 inch long catkins festooning the branches of the silver birch, the leaf buds still brown. One of the most striking sights is the Norway maple Goldworth Purple, with erect lime-green flowers merging, or is it contrasting, with the rich, copper-coloured leaves as they unfold. Each spring it takes my breath away with its elegance. A chestnut has young candles, as yet only 3 inches tall but full of expectation. The pear tree, probably 200 years old, is white with flowers and has its traditional blackbird in residence. Out of sight, but within smelling distance, are two balsam poplars with red catkins and deliciously scented sticky buds. I wish we had an alder, the golden-leafed variety with yellow catkins. I have wanted one ever since I saw it as the principal feature in a small town garden. The wild crabs and geans in the hedgerows are at their best, and so are the bullace, sloes and other wild plums.

*     *     *          *     *     *          *     *     *

The moles had moved in overnight. "They do say if you tie a worm to the trap you'll catch him," said my 79 year old gardener, Fred, as we stood together appraising the patch he had dug and dunged ready for the autumn fruiting strawberries. But his recommendation was to do nothing until the moles had eaten the feast of worms he had dug in with the dung; they would move on and he could firm the soil once more. As usual, with his unruffled common sense, he was right. These moles are a problem, undermining the roots of any plants they meet. I am sure ours are of ancient lineage, dating from the days of ridge and furrow cultivation, for that is where they come from, judging by the molehills which make their way towards our vegetable garden. You can either trap them or drive them away with smoke bombs; one thing I have learnt from experience is that the best place to set the trap is near the end of a newly-made run. I caught one like this the other day. If you have caught nothing within 24 hours, you must move your trap on. I have been searching through the old writers for advice and found an appealing thought in Thomas Hill's *Profitable Arte of Gardening* of 1568. Put a live mole into a "deape earthen potte, set unto the edge in the earth". The mole "after a whyle feeling himself thus enclosed will crie out" whereupon all the moles in the area will hear him and "hastely draw near, minding to help him". After that there is no problem; they will all be prisoners in the "earthenpotte". All I want now is a live mole to act as a decoy and get me started.

\* \* \*      \* \* \*      \* \* \*

The predominant colour for hedgerow flowers in spring

is white. Elderflowers open in mid-June and are creamy white, with a delicious heady scent. Put a bunch in your horse's bridle and this will help to keep the flies away when you are riding. For the larder, one of the best cooling drinks can be made from elderflowers. It is quick and easy to make as long as you remember to buy some tartaric acid. All you need to do is to pick a bucketful of flowerheads (about 25), slice a lemon and four oranges, add three pints of cold water, three pounds of white sugar and 2 oz of tartaric acid. Mix them all together and leave to stand for two days, remembering to stir whenever you go past. Then strain the liquid into clean bottles. Dilute it as you use it, but as it will not keep more than a week or two, enjoy it and be generous with it. A spoonful splashed over your ripe strawberries and raspberries will give them an extra piquancy, a muscatel-like flavour.

* * *　　* * *　　* * *

One curious effect of the May downpours has been the behaviour of the bees on our doormat. The stone canopy over our garden door crashed during last winter's frost with the result that even when the shutters are closed the water seeps in and drenches the new doormat. When I open the shutters after a wet night, the bees are waiting. They arrive in their tens and alight on the mat—real coconut—and apparently enjoy some delicious goody secreted in the matting. There they stay, paying no attention to my comings and goings. I wish I knew what they are after.

# JUNE

That wonderful garden raconteur, Canon Ellacombe, always full of sound advice and country common sense, must have been enjoying a good lunch with a bowl of scented roses on his dining-table on the day in June 1871 when he wrote: "Is there any other month in the year that can show such a delightful triplet as we have now—roses, strawberries and green peas?" We all have our own June speciality without which we would feel something was missing. My broad beans have been in advance of the peas this year and thanks to the Mediterranean weather the early potatoes and strawberries were a treat before May was out. As for roses, the first sweetly-scented blooms have been *Souvenir de la Malmaison* and *Zéphirine Drouhin*. This is the season when it is most difficult to go away even for a night—there is so much to be done at home. But when we do manage to get away there are always rewards. Driving from home through to the eastern counties in late May it seemed as though England was a land of white lilacs and pink and white May trees; every front garden and hedgerow were heavy with blossom. The fields of oil-seed rape glowed like brightest sunshine. At home I wake to the cuckoo, the milking machine or a particularly noisy aeroplane which sounds as though it is coming right into the house most mornings at 4 a.m. When we were staying in Dorset I thought I was dreaming when peacocks calling to each other disturbed my sleep. I remembered Ruskin's thought "that the most beautiful things in the world are the most useless; peacocks and lilies for instance." I don't necessarily agree with the sentiment but so far have managed to stand out against the introduction of peacocks to our garden — they may be beautiful but are also destructive. Lilies are a different matter.

    * * *     * * *     * * *

We all feel sometimes that things are not as good as they used to be but luckily it often works the other way. Plants brought in from the wild and cultivated in richer soil improve in character, becoming part of our borders or popular house plants. Mignonette, *Reseda odorata*, however, has been contrary. Seeds were sent to Philip Miller in 1752 at the Chelsea Physic Garden. He says in his *Gardener's Dictionary:* "The flowers... produced in long spikes... smell very like fresh raspberries, which occasions its being much cultivated in the English gardens." Half a century later Napoleon sent seeds from Egypt to the Empress Josephine. The flowers were scented and soon it became the fashion in France to grow mignonette (nicknamed "Little Darling") in pots and to stand these on balconies to perfume the air on the occasion of smart Parisian soirees. In 19th century England mignonette was a regular cottage-garden plant, grown especially for its

60

scent, and William Robinson reported that "the compact strong garden variety 'Machet' is the kind grown so largely in pots for the London market." Yet one seldom sees mignonette grown here today. The simple answer is its lost scent but it has a firm history and should be pursued. A kind friend to whom I frequently turn for advice went to Egypt in March and I alerted him to try to find wild Egyptian mignonette. He came home saying that as every square yard is cultivated there was no hope of success. Every time I see seed offered for sale I buy it, hoping that one day I will be rewarded with a delicious whiff of that unexpected raspberry scent. Now it has happened at last. At the Philadelphia Flower Show in March last year I bought a packet of *Reseda odorata* seeds. We sowed them this spring and by the second week of June I had two trays of raspberry-scented flowers waiting to be planted out. Some will go into beds beside the house, by the kitchen and drawing-room doors and at other strategic places where scent is a pleasure. A few will go into pots so that they can be brought indoors to perfume the house, but most important of all I must remember to harvest the seeds so that we have a plentiful supply for next year. It would be exciting to make mignonette a favourite garden and pot plant once more. Our next search will be for a scented musk plant *(Mimulus moschata)* to propagate.

❖ ❖ ❖      ❖ ❖ ❖      ❖ ❖ ❖

Has the hawthorn blossom along our lanes ever been

better? It has brought comments of amazement and appreciation from Americans I have talked to during their visits to England this month. This has brought home to me the huge numbers of these bushes there are growing in our hedgerows and in clumps in windswept corners of fields where they act as windbreaks for sheep, cattle and horses. Most of them have doubtless been sown by the birds, eating and digesting the hips in autumn. The cow parsley under the hawthorn looks spectacular, too, in beautiful lacy drifts. It will soon be superseded by ox-eye daisies and blue geraniums. The cow parsley has so many local names it must grow in every county of England. Here we call it Queen Anne's Lace or Lady's Needlework, much more alluring titles than Devil's Oatmeal as in Yorkshire or Cow-Mumble (East Anglia). But I like the Irish name of Gypsy's Umbrella. Whatever it is called, it looks delicate and lovely with the sun shining through it on days when the earth is warm, the air is cool. The effect is of mist rising, and a rainbow should appear on the horizon at any moment.

\* \* \*      \* \* \*      \* \* \*

This is the month when the trees with their fresh newly-opened leaves make a beautiful tapestry effect of soft and varying greens. Nature is so clever and gives us a serial display, starting with the hedgerow sallows in early spring, going through the hazel and alder, chestnut and sycamore, elder and crab apples, and ending with oak

and ash. Perhaps the last to open their leaves are the mulberry and acacia. One acacia in my garden, grown from seed we picked off the ground in the Botanic garden in Madrid at least a quarter of a century ago, is only just (June 12) showing enough signs of growth to be seen silhouetted against a changing cloudy sky. This is where my resident chaffinch sits throughout the summer. It is a pity June does not last twice as long (we could do without January) both for its beauty and for the enticing events which happen regularly and are advertised for all to see along the roadside. This weekend we had a choice of national ride and drive, celebrity cricket match and polo.

¤ ¤ ¤          ¤ ¤ ¤          ¤ ¤ ¤

An unwelcome bird visitor we have had recently is a hungry heron. In 1954 we put three goldfish in our pond and these had multiplied an hundredfold. They were utterly fearless of humans and as soon as they sensed footsteps would gather in a phalanx for food. As their numbers dwindled we stupidly did not immediately suspect a heron; then one midday I saw him from my window, gliding down. He has left us only ten fish but perhaps these will increase as the others did. Inevitably this has led to heron thoughts. Quite the best comes from John Ford, father of Anna, who once owned a stretch of trout stream in Cumberland. One of his fisherman friends was Arthur Severn, who, when his cousin John Ruskin died leaving him a legacy, developed the now famous trout hatcheries at Bibury. Arthur Severn understood the attraction herons have for fish. A heron will wade in where the water is shallow and patiently wait for the fish to gather round him. Severn's theory was that their legs gave off an oil attractive to fish, so being a practical man he shot one and cut off its legs. He boiled these to make an oily paste into which he could dip his trout flies. Not quite cricket, you may think, and Arthur Severn is dead so we cannot ask him. All we can do is surround our small pond with a trip wire which I hope will not deter the garden birds from taking their daily baths from the waterlilies' leaves.

❖ ❖ ❖          ❖ ❖ ❖          ❖ ❖ ❖

As a child I was told rather severely to "use my eyes" if I had been clumsy or failed to find something I had been sent to fetch. Then suddenly it all changed, somebody realised what was wrong. I was near (short) sighted. In class we had to copy from the blackboard the first few verses of the Ballad of Sir Patrick Spens, the best sailor who ever sailed the seas. I already knew the poem by heart as Sir Patrick was an ancestor of my mother and I was extremely proud of the fact. Alas, my spelling was rotten and the verses which I had so joyously 'copied' were copiously corrected in red ink. Luckily the mistress recognised my problem and I was sent off to the oculist. This happened nearly sixty years ago but I can remember vividly looking through my new spectacles for the first time at the world around me. I walked into the school playground and it was literally an eye-opener. Things seemed smaller but incredibly clear and well defined. In the country what a lot one misses without reasonable eyesight. A friend who has recently had a cataract operation described to me how bright the white daisies on the lawn suddenly appeared to him. His dark moss-green motorcar became bright cerulean blue. The blues in his flower borders were far more intense than he had ever seen them before. Shades that had been a rusty brown were now bright red. As he looked into the faces of the flowers he could see the individual petals of each bloom. After our conversation I took off my spectacles and walked round the garden and was surprised how changed the total effect of each border became. The small shapes no longer mattered. It was the general outline and the weight of the colours that became important, rather than the detail.

\* \* \*     \* \* \*     \* \* \*

We all talk about the weather. In April when the sun was shining, if you remarked on what a lovely day it was the answer came back: "Yes, but it's too cold." In June you rarely hear country people complain about the rain. It is the growing season, wonderful for corn and grass crops. But the fields around us, where milking cows are grazing and constantly on the move, have become too muddy and the cows have been kept inside at night to prevent more trampling of grass, spoiling their own food.

None of this agrees with the rhyme of the oak and the ash. This spring the oak was much sooner into leaf than the ash so by rights we should have been due a splash. But we've had a soak already. The major result so far has been a lack of balmy June evenings. The nights have been cold, but despite this the rate of growth on our road verges has been fast. This long grass acts as shelter and hiding-place for many of the young animals and birds that are about now. I always associate June with the many newly-hatched birds that are so tame and allow one to approach quite close to them in the garden. One family of tits that have just hatched out are in a temporary crevice in a wall where building is under way and coping stones are due to be put on. The builders will have to wait now until the tits have flown. Our garden is a haven for shrews which live in the drystone walls, and this week there is a family of tame fieldmice in one of the borders.

🐦 🐦 🐦          🐦 🐦 🐦          🐦 🐦 🐦

As summer comes around I am always on the lookout for cooking receipts with a difference, using plants from my garden and from the countryside as ingredients. It is annoying when you find that you are just too late and the flower you need has gone past its best. Now it is too late to make dandelion wine but there is plenty of time for elderflower champagne. What about alpine strawberry soup? Boil three cups of strawberries in three cups of water, thicken this with arrowroot and serve it as a cold

67

summer soup topped with a spoonful of yoghurt. There are still plenty of stinging nettles about—if you can find young leaves, so much the better. When you are making a quiche filling try adding chopped and boiled dandelion or nettle leaves to your mixture to give colour and a distinctive flavour. Flower fritters are good. For each one you need one flower or flower cluster to dip into batter. In past years I have used day-lily flowers but this summer I hope to try elderflowers, rose petals, nasturtiums and even acacia blossom. Rose-petal syrup is delicious poured over vanilla ice-cream. You can make a store of this, using maple syrup mixed in equal quantities with rose petals. Bring them slowly to the boil, then allow them to stand until the next day. Strain and use immediately or keep it in an airtight jar. One of the best summer sorbets is made from blackcurrant leaves. Later on in the summer when the *rugosa* hips are ripe and red, gather a panful, chop them and simmer in just enough water to cover them. If you have time mash the hips to bring out the maximum flavour and vitamins and then allow to cool and stand overnight before you strain the mixture. Warm this and add a few spoonfuls of honey or maple syrup before you bottle it.

# JULY

With mid-day temperatures up in the 80s I become limp like the fast-fading flowers in the garden and unable to do anything active. So I must resort to early rising before the sun gets too high, which means adjusting my internal clock. It is amazing how much more one gets through when no one else is about to interrupt actions or trains of thought, when no telephone or door-bell rings and even the letters are left lying as they fell when the postman pushed them through the letter-box.

By ten o'clock I have done a full morning's work and can enjoy a feeling of achievement. The stillness of the early morning scene enables me to take in and enjoy many things which pass me by during the bustle of the day. First there are the scents, which seem even more generous with their offerings than they are in the evening. The good old-fashioned dog-rose in the hedgerow was almost effusive in its fragrance and the leaves of the Sweetbriar or Eglantine, so loved by the Elizabethans, had a richness, which must have been caused by the dew, far surpassing anything they usually provide, except after rain. The soil in the lane is so parched even the nettles are fading, but the limestone walls seem to enjoy the sun's warmth which they wisely store and give off in the darkness to any nearby living thing. One morning I met the neighbouring cats who were prowling round looking for nests and listening for the cheeps of the tender young birds. They were threatened with my hosepipe and I hope they will now cease to prowl for a few days; one of them had already torn down a perfect nest we had been watching, made by a familiar family of goldfinches for their fledglings. The birds have much to learn, the hard way; in future I hope they will build high, where the cats cannot climb. Two or three nests ruined in this way can destroy the natural balance of birds in the garden. I would hate to be without the goldfinches pecking away at the seed-heads in autumn. We have left a row of lettuces, the pink-leafed ones, which were too pretty to pull up and are now a mass of seeds, which is providing much happiness for them. Another intriguing discovery I made was the offering of the teasels. Their stem-clasping leaves are perfoliate – united together at the stem – and thus with their upright habit they create a perfect receptacle to store rainwater and dew. Each pair of leaves is arranged alternately and grows so accurately that when the water overflows from one pair of leaves it is caught by the awaiting cup formed by the next. In dry weather this store must be a boon to thirsty insects and smaller birds. The mechanism is so neatly designed it could well be the prototype for a delicate garden fountain.

✾ ✾ ✾     ✾ ✾ ✾     ✾ ✾ ✾

I expect the policy of cutting the roadside verges varies in each county but I have noticed round here, especially in the smaller lanes, that the grass has been left uncut long enough for many of the wild flowers and grasses to go to seed. This is all good news and augurs well for next year's crop of wild flowers. The past few days of midsummer's hot sunshine have helped to bring forward the ripening of the seeds. I have noticed in particular the mauve and yellow vetches, poppies, pastel blue scabious, blue geranium, ragged robin, campion and convolvulus, ladies' bedstraw and tall spikes of verbascum. In most places only a narrow strip has been cut, just sufficient to improve driving visibility on the winding lanes. When you drive slowly you have the opportunity to enjoy the flowers. In some places I have been fascinated by the variety of tall umbelliferous plants. In the days of carriages and traps travellers sat high enough to see over the top of the roadside vegetation, so there was no need to cut it for safety and anyway the council roadmen had only their scythes to work with. Our motorways and bypasses are straight enough, so the tall grasses in no way obscure our vision while driving. Last summer on a central section of a bypass near here there was a remarkable crop of dianthus. This year they have spread and are even better —good news indeed.

\* \* \*      \* \* \*      \* \* \*

My bees in the roof have been exceptionally active recently, and I have learnt a lot about them. A swarm of bees in May is worth a load of hay, quite valuable in fact,

73

but a swarm in June is only worth a silver spoon. Considering all we have read about bee colonies having been killed by the severe winter I should think that even a July swarm would be welcomed by bee-keepers whose hives are empty. Ours waited until the very hot weather was over and on June 25th, a warm, sunny and still day, made their first sortie. Since then they have kept us wondering how many more swarms will appear. The first swarm landed on the *Alchemilla mollis* in front of the house and very soon was like a large black puddle on the paving. My worry was that garden visitors — and there were more than 200 that day — would be so occupied with plants that they would not notice them. A charming Japanese photographer got closest to this while he was looking up at the climbing plants growing on the house. However, while they are swarming the bees are so laden with honey and bent upon following the queen that they are quite harmless to humans, unless of course we do something foolish. I had no idea how to deal with the swarm on the ground but luck was on my side and I recognised a man who I knew kept bees, walking round the garden. No problem, he said, and he put a large cardboard box gently over the swarm. By evening they were quiet and settled and my bee friend came back and collected them. I thought this would be the end of the story, but not a bit of it. Obviously the weather was just right for swarming, not too hot and not heavy or sultry, and around noon on several successive days the familiar buzzing would start up. There would be a cloud of bees flying around the eaves of the house close to their home, then they would move off in a frenzied but ordered manner and for a few moments the air would be thick with them. The scout bee had done his reconnoitring and they would land on their favourite spot, a branch of the smoke tree close by. They did this on at least five days. They would hang there for a while and then take off, one swarm flying towards the village and another making off over the garden wall and away into the fields. I hope they found a good home. These are Italian bees and are very hardy. On other occasions they went back into the roof. I asked my bee friend why there were so many queens and learnt that he thought there must be several colonies in the rafters, unlike in a hive, where there will only be one queen.

\* \* \*     \* \* \*     \* \* \*

"Is there a green in your village?" I was asked recently by a traveller. Sadly, the answer is no, nor do we have a duckpond, but we do have a cricket ground tucked away inside the park walls. In our village there is nowhere a green could have developed naturally. Our village, small as it is, has always been on a main thoroughfare—in fact two. The Romans chose a site here between two of their important roads. Centuries later it was the point at which two roads intersected; one from Gloucester to London, the other from Cirencester to Oxford. When the turnpike was made in 1753 it gave a greater importance to the village street, which avoided the turnpike for the locals and it was at this time and also in the early 19th century that the squire built estate cottages. This all culminated in the fact that we now have no village green on which to meet and gossip on summer evenings. The village green needed no mowing when the local inhabitants could graze their geese, fattening them for Michaelmas, and tether their horses there. This kept down the grass and provided natural manure for their gardens. The duckpond is a mixed blessing for though it makes an artistic feature it can create an unwanted mess with ducks puddling in wet weather and with dried cracked earth in summer. But I wish we had a village green, one with well-made seats all round.

ɛ ɛ ɛ          ɛ ɛ ɛ          ɛ ɛ ɛ

When Lord Beeching reduced our railway system by closing a network of local lines I am sure he was unaware of some of the side-effects. The trains bringing passengers from Swindon let off a shrill whistle as they approached Cirencester. If we could hear it in our village it meant that the wind was in the west and this was a harbinger of rain. Another train went chuffing through the countryside, crossing farm roads and field cuttings. The north-east wind carried this sound to us and then we knew we were in for a dry cold spell. Now we have to rely on the weather-man or the telephone service for our information, unless we are up and about at six o'clock and see the rooks flying directly away into the distance. Then we are sure of a fine day. If they just spiral round about, we can expect rain, especially if the cats are playing and the cows lying down in their chosen positions.

❋ ❋ ❋          ❋ ❋ ❋          ❋ ❋ ❋

Nearly 20 years ago my husband was given a small hamper full of glass photographic plates. He discovered that these all dated back to the 1890s and the turn of the century. He had several of them blown up to poster size and used them to cover the walls of one of the rooms in Arlington Mill, the museum he created in Bibury. Recently my daughter has had contact prints made of many more of them, especially those taken in our own village. Many interesting facts emerge. The first and most obvious is their excellent quality, both in composition and clarity. The cottages have changed but little; in fact if it were not for the television aerials they would look the same. The road was not of tarmac and looked white. The paths had pretty grass edgings instead of kerbstones and the quiet of the village is made apparent by the groups of children playing in the street with no fear of lorries thundering by.

＊ ＊ ＊          ＊ ＊ ＊          ＊ ＊ ＊

This is the season for picnics, when the weather is set fair and the ground quite dry; little rain has fallen with us for weeks. It is perfect to spread out the rug on a newly-mown field and to sit back for a while and feel you are part of the countryside, smelling the grass and the hedge-rows and listening to the sounds of the insects around you.

You may find yourself sharing a hamper full of exotic food and sparkling champagne in the peace and beauty of the Glyndbourne garden, the music of the first act still ringing in your ears. It matters not that you are surrounded by other picnickers, for they are integrated into the garden, hidden by hedges and borders and experiencing the same pleasures. This is the grandest kind of picnic, when the tablecloth is laid with silver spoons and crystal goblets; it is an evening to remember for its 18th century touch. In contrast, when the spirit moves you, at a moment's notice you may gather up a slice of bread, wash a lettuce, hard-boil an egg, fill a bottle with newly-made elderflower cordial and settle at the end of your own garden or some-body else's — unpack your basket and enjoy the solitude of the countryside where you cannot hear the telephone ringing. As you travel through Europe there are the picnics you look forward to ravenously. Before setting off in the morning your picnic basket has been filled with delicious fare from the local delicatessen and bakery and with bottles of vin du pays. As lunchtime draws near you drive slowly, keeping your eyes open for the ideal site, a place with a wonderful view, some shade and enough flat ground to set up your folding table and chairs. These are easy to take on the roof rack. It is essential at this kind of picnic to sit at a table, with plates and knives to cut and spread your bread and pâté. If you have left your table at home, then you find a quiet churchyard with a suitable table tomb. Years ago we always had family picnics, with girls and whippets piled into the car, fetching boys from school and then on to Windsor Great Park where we set out rugs and baskets under the same favourite oak tree. In winter there was hot soup and baked potatoes, in summer cold chicken and cooling drinks—all much more fun and relaxing than any hotel meal. In winter there was also a walk to keep us warm and ripe chestnuts to find; in summer we had the wild flowers to discover, clambering through the high bracken.

# AUGUST

The local flower show was great fun, with lovely dahlias, long carrots, solid cabbages, pansies with delightful faces as well as large, mop-headed chrysanthemums. The flower arrangements showed plenty of imagination and, I thought, so did the people who had compiled the competitions, for without creative classes there will not be good entries. There proved to be much scope in the class entitled 'A nursery rhyme' when Little Boy Blue and the Old Lady who lived in a Shoe appeared in well-chosen floral form. While the tug-of-war was going on and the rain threatened we watched small children on fat ponies negotiating painted fences. But the best value for me, a chance visitor, was undoubtedly the dog show. The majority were family pets but I spotted a few who had been taught ring behaviour. When under the scrutiny of the judge they held their pose like Hollywood children awaiting the photographer. Those without this discipline demonstrated their fondness for the family when they saw them at the ringside. It was the diverse range of shapes and sizes that gave me such pleasure and must surely have presented the judge with a serious problem. The smallest was an obviously highly intelligent border terrier, a good ratter, I was sure. There was a mystery black dog which looked like a soft black shawl, so well draped that no one could really see what its feet were doing. The lurchers were graceful and the Dobermans well groomed and fit, but it was the Pyrenean mountain dog that I would like to have been given. I had a chat with its owner who explained how these Blaireau dogs act as guards for sheep in the mountains. Perhaps in his native country Ben would have taken on a fiercer attitude but here on show he was deceptively gentle.

❀ ❀ ❀    ❀ ❀ ❀    ❀ ❀ ❀

The first week in August we had the regular arrival of thunderbugs. I do not know their proper names but they are very small and black, and although they do not appear to bite or cause any other damage, they are extremely irritating when they alight on one, crawling through the hair and generally disturbing one's occupation and conversation. Some years they are worse than others, depending on the weather, but always they appear on warm still days. I try putting sprigs of rue and other strong-smelling herbs behind my ears but the best antidote is to wear a large-brimmed hat. Their presence reminds me to look for other insects that are busy among the flowers. I was taking an American landscape architect round the garden and as we passed the hostas he commented on the lack of holes in their leaves. He assumed that slugs are not so omnipresent in this country as in his; maybe he is right. When his rich clients complain to him about their holey hostas his firm reply is: "You must eat and let eat, live and let live."

It is remarkable how the colours in the pattern of the countryside change almost daily during the time of harvest. You notice this when driving through the Cotswolds, where the contours of the land allow you to see miles around you and you become aware that most of the fields are cultivated for corn. As the days of the harvest get closer so the view changes from green to golden and except for the few grass fields the whole panorama becomes a glowing yellow. But it is only for a few days. As parts of the patchwork are harvested so, almost immediately, they are ploughed, preparing for next year's crop and the patches of gold become brown. Gone are the days when the corn was cut and bound into sheaves which the harvesters then stacked tidily into stooks. With the same number of sheaves to each stook the pattern was as regular as if it had been drawn out on paper, measured and copied. Seen on a sunlit evening the slanting shadows of each stook added another dimension to the already beautiful pattern. But I am day-dreaming back to the days (not so long ago) of the binder and threader, horses and carts.

꿈 꿈 꿈          꿈 꿈 꿈          꿈 꿈 꿈

The pair of green woodpeckers living just outside our garden have been yaffling joyously recently. They discovered several ants' nests which we had uncovered in a pathway where we had been pulling up straggling rock roses. For a day or two they were so intent on their occupation that they paid little attention to humans passing by.

It was fascinating watching them, first probing with their bills then catching the ants with their amazingly long tongues, moving them so fast as to be almost invisible. Thank goodness I had not immediately smothered the ants' nests in poison. Both woodpeckers were busy collecting enough food to make a regurgitated meal for their young. When disturbed the birds watched from a nearby pear tree, coming back as soon as the coast was clear. We have had green woodpeckers about in the garden for many years and presumably they are the same pair or their offspring. What surprised me most was the speed with which the birds spotted the ants' nests. They could not possibly have seen them from the air, so do they immediately home in on likely spots where vegetation has been disturbed? They have done a very thorough job of removing every vestige of the nests.

\* \* \*        \* \* \*        \* \* \*

Benedict Williams and I were chatting about trees and hedges as we clipped back the Golden King hollies one warm August morning. Benedict has a nursery which specialises in hollies so he comes twice a year to collect our holly clippings to use as cuttings in his mist propagator. He grows 20 different varieties and they make good quick-growing hedges, putting on at least a foot of growth each year. They have many advantages including a lovely leaf-lustre. They stay well-clothed right to the ground and are admirable town shrubs as well as putting up with sea air. They make an impenetrable barrier and can be clipped to any shape you choose. John Evelyn in his *Silva, or Discourse of Forest Trees*, extols the virtues of holly, as well he might for his garden was ruined during the tenancy of the Czar of Muscovy, except for his 400 ft. long, 9 ft. high and 5 ft. diameter 'impregnable' holly hedge 'glittering with its armed and varnished leaves'.

A hedge of holly, thieves that would invade
Repulses like a growing palisade.

He explains how his original planting used five or six quickthorn to every holly. As these grew the quickthorn was pulled up to make space for the holly. The timber, he says, is hard and valuable. It was used by millwrights and engravers and also makes the best handles for tools, doorbars and bolts. Recently I was walking in a garden overlooking a remote Cotswold valley. A windbreak hedge fitted perfectly into the landscape; it was a tapestry of deciduous trees: quickset or hawthorn with oak and sycamore interspersed. Our host explained how he had used existing trees, cut and laid them and infilled with seedling thorns. In spring he said the colour of the young oak leaves is breathtakingly beautiful. In summer it looked lovely too.

❀ ❀ ❀          ❀ ❀ ❀          ❀ ❀ ❀

I felt very depressed after a conversation with one of my neighbours. He is the owner of several hundred acres, much of it grazing land but with some woodland. Running through it is a river along which is a public right of way. He is very concerned about the manner in which a small percentage of the people who use the path abuse it. Why is litter inevitable? If one cigarette is left in a packet, the packet goes back into a pocket, so why not if it is empty? People even remove stones from my neighbour's walls, presumably to make walls somewhere else. Adjoining covers are walked through, disturbing the game, and poachers who take fish from the river plead ignorance when caught. This is a problem; how is one to educate townspeople to the fact that they must treat the countryside with respect? Exhibitions in school might be of some help but it is probably a perennial problem to which there is no satisfactory solution.

    ﻼ ﻼ ﻼ        ﻼ ﻼ ﻼ        ﻼ ﻼ ﻼ

When I came down to breakfast on a recent Sunday morning I found a barefoot visitor in his bathrobe walking in the garden. The dew was thick on the ground and he was admiring the drops of water in the alchemilla leaves. He was not English, nor a farmer, and his first question was to ask why there was so much straw lying about on the lawn. At first I was perplexed, too, and then realised it must be some nearby farmer straw burning and the wind had carried a lot of unburnt straw in my direction. Cause and effect is often a surprise and I am sure the farmer was unaware of the results of his work.

Ideas often go in cycles and when I asked an Oxfordshire farmer if he burnt his straw his answer was "No". He explained that his workers are delighted not to do so. Ploughing it in causes them extra work but they feel they are on the right path.

# SEPTEMBER

The weeks of September and early October have always
been among my favourites in the year. Twenty-five
years ago it was getting up to exercise the horses, fat and
shiny-coated, just up from grass. All summer long the
stables had echoed emptiness but by September there
were warm straw beds, oats in the manger and alert
friendly heads watching every movement over the stable
doors. It was a slow job getting them ready for hunting
—no good hurrying it or you would end up with a load
of trouble. A week or two of walking, to tone up gradually
muscles and our own, then regular trotting on the hard
high road, and later we were into the fields for the first
canter. Hilly country is a bonus and we are lucky to have
our grassy Cotswold banks. Uphill for wind and downhill
for muscle is a sure maxim and by the time the first hunting days came round one was smugly satisfied that all the
careful preparation had paid off and you felt the muscle
and strength and enthusiasm beneath you. For me, that
was years ago and now September has a different but
equally alluring charm. The urgency is over. It happens
almost overnight; the berries ripen, the garden defies
attention—too late to introduce extra colours to the
borders and too early to put them all to bed for winter.
So I can sit back and enjoy it all, perhaps making some

constructive plans but always postponing my activities until later. Often these days have a stillness that is unique — not a rustle of wind, early morning mists that mask the distant trees, red apples hanging on as long as they can, until ready for storing. This year our quince crop is terrific, every branch hanging low with the weight of the downy but hard fruit. We will know when they are ready for picking by their strong scent; outside, this is quite pleasant, but a large basketful waiting in the larder makes an almost nauseous smell. They are like gold; not one must be wasted. We must cut them, boil them, strain them through muslin and make them into a fine clear amber jelly. The autumn hedgerows are bountiful, too, bursting with fruit for picking. There are sloes for sloe gin, hips, haws, elderberries and crab-apples for jellies, to be carefully labelled and stored for the winter. The taste of elderberries on their own has no subtlety but mixed with other things they can add a richness of flavour and colour. Another of my favourite jellies is made from the small grapes of our Strawberry Vine. Years ago, Vita Sackville-West recommended it and added that one could buy the vine from Clarence Elliott, Joe Elliott's father. We have never regretted buying ours; planted with its roots outside and climbing under an open verandah roof, it produces a prolific crop each autumn.

\* \* \*  \* \* \*  \* \* \*

Rosebay willow is beautiful in the wild but a menace in

the garden. Each September, its appearance reminds me of one day when I was seven. A friend and I had been allowed to roam alone on the dunes behind Walmer Castle in Kent. This wonderful willowherb was growing in profusion as tall as we were; we picked armfuls, some in flower and some with ripening seeds, and as we walked home through the garden, each with a cherished bouquet, we met the gardener. At the time I could not understand his dismay as hundreds of seeds went wafting into his weedless borders. Now when I see its deceptively pretty pink flowers appearing in my borders I remember that carefree day and pull it out, roots and all. Autumn is the time to harvest seeds of our special flowers; plants such as *Nicotiana sylvestris*, to my mind the sweetest-scented of the tobacco family, and the nasty-smelling *Salvia sclaria* var. *turkestanica*, whose mauve bracts last for weeks and always cause comments of approval; all those which are hard to find in the seedsmen's catalogues. We should follow Thomas Tusser's 16th century advice in his poem on points of good husbandry:

Good huswifes in summer will save their own seedes,
Against the next years, as occasion needes.
One seed for another, to make an exchange,
With fellowlie neighbourhood seemeth not strange.

   🌿 🌿 🌿      🌿 🌿 🌿      🌿 🌿 🌿

Perhaps it is more difficult to be a good neighbour

in the country than in a town. I don't just mean being friendly. I mean positively not taking away the early morning sun from the next-door garden by planting trees, particularly fast-growing evergreens. A friend of mine did this about ten years ago when an adjoining old house was converted into flats with windows overlooking her garden. "What can I plant?" she said. "We can't have them peering at us through the windows." So fast-growing Leylandii went in. Now they are fairly ugly and nobody wants them as the nearer, slower-growing trees do the work, so out they will all come. Fired by these thoughts early yesterday morning when the September sun was still low in the sky, I went to look at the cottage garden beyond my western boundary. My garden was bathed in sun and warmth, the cottage garden cool and sunless and it felt like being in a different climate, so cut off was it by my tall trees, two limes, a copper beech and an evergreen oak. Cutting down mature trees is not a thing to do without weighing up all the factors involved. Their removal would let light and early morning sun into the neighbouring garden but it would also let in the east wind. I would have an unwanted view of the village and the west wind could rush into my garden; but worst of all I would no longer have my sound-barrier against the main-road traffic. The adjoining garden belongs to my daughter so she will probably win.

❖ ❖ ❖      ❖ ❖ ❖      ❖ ❖ ❖

Had I seen a photograph or picture 20 years ago of the September landscape with huge round bales dotted across the stubble fields, my reaction would have been a feeling of unreality. Today this surrealist view has become a reality. The mere fact of their weight and volume represents strength. If I shut my eyes I can imagine an avalanche of them rolling, steadily at first, then gathering speed and rushing down a sloping field until stopped by a hedge or high wall. How do they get picked up? Or are they rolled along? Why are they better than the old conventional square bales? How much do they weigh and are they easy to handle and finally use? A few minutes' conversation with the owner of a field of these bales has answered my questions. As the baler has to stop before it can eject each bale, it can also turn into such a position as to ensure that the bale has its flat side towards the slope and will not start to roll away. Being round they can easily shed water. They weigh about 5 cwt. and as long as the right equipment is used they are easy to move and store. In winter, when used as fodder, they fit into specially designed containers or racks for the cattle to chew away at. Used for bedding, they should unwind as they are rolled.

\* \* \*　　　\* \* \*　　　\* \* \*

You will always know if hedgehogs have been in your garden because they leave their droppings on the lawn. I can almost track their nightly walkabouts. They are among the good creatures which inhabit our gardens, eating many of the bad creatures. It distresses me when I see flattened corpses on the road, the result of a night accident. If only they had a few luminous spines to show up in car headlights, they would be much safer. Another death trap is a pond with no escape route. Ours is like that and I have a guilty conscience about it. One morning we were early enough to rescue a large hedgehog which must have toppled in, intent on a drink. Recently I had the pleasure of meeting Sue and Leo Stocker and one of their tame hedgehogs. They are a remarkable couple who have started the Wildlife Hospitals Trust, to give help to all kinds of British wildlife. They will take in casualties, treat them and return them to the wild, with a particular emphasis on sensible releasing so that the animals have a chance to rehabilitate. At the moment Sue and Leo are fund-raising to build Europe's first wildlife teaching hospital where they will have the opportunity to pass on much of the valuable knowledge they have gained while handling sick and wounded animals. Their St. Tiggy-winkle's Hedgehog Fact Sheet is full of intriguing hedgehog knowledge. The babies are born without spines and when these eventually grow, they are white—the brown ones develop later. Their favourite diet is caterpillars and beetles, closely followed by slugs and worms. They enjoy a saucer of tinned dog or cat food, which is much better for them than bread and milk. Slug pellets poison them when they eat dead slugs so if you value hedgehogs in your garden, please do not put down slug pellets. If you

94

want to know more about the Wildlife Hospitals Trust, write to Leo Stocker at 1 Pemberton Close, Aylesbury, Buckinghamshire. You will be surprised at the extent of the work they do but naturally more funds are always needed.

# OCTOBER

The western wind has blown but a few days
Yet the first leaf already flies from the bough.
On the drying paths I walk in my thin shoes;
In the first cold I have donned my quilted coat.

This is Arthur Waley's translation of a Chinese poem.
The western wind has blown here for several days
bringing the leaves tumbling, but it is the wind from the
east and north that sends me indoors to don my quilted
jacket. The temperature is so changeable that one must
be equipped for anything. At one moment the day is
thunderous; a few moments later there is hardly a cloud
to be seen, the sun is warm on my back and just as quickly
my mood can change. But as for thin shoes, wellingtons
are surely more useful. If I need to wear my quilted coat
then it is time for some tender plants to be given a layer
of bracken or an extra mulch, or to be taken indoors for
the winter. We know what time the sun will set and when
the clocks are put back but what is always unknown is
when the first frost will assail us. We must be prepared.

\* \* \*        \* \* \*          \* \* \*

Our hedgerows have interesting tales to tell. The theory
put forward by Dr. Max Hooper is that the age of a hedge

can be measured by the number of tree and shrub species in it. In approximate terms, every different species contained within 100 ft. of hedgerow represents 100 years of growth. The research fund of the Society of Antiquaries has made a grant for a project to survey hedges in certain parishes in Gloucestershire. The work is being done by students of the Institute of Archaeology, University of London, under the guidance of Richard Reece. Taryn Nixon has analysed 158 hedges in our parish. She has found 24 species growing, with hawthorn, elder, ash, blackthorn and hazel each being present in at least two or three of the hedges. The interesting historical fact that emerges is that the two hedges which according to this theory should be pre-Norman, enclose the old ridge and furrow fields and are on a line with the oldest known road.

❋ ❋ ❋         ❋ ❋ ❋         ❋ ❋ ❋

Living in a part of the country where houses and field boundaries are all built of stone and where it is a rarity to see a redbrick house, I am conscious of the subtle changes in the colour and mellowness of the buildings. As we travelled from home to Yorkshire and back via Lincolnshire recently we more or less covered that part of the Jurassic limestone belt running from the Cotswolds through to the Yorkshire coast. Our own honey-coloured oolitic limestone gradually changes in Warwickshire where the blue lias is grey rather than blue. We have a piece of Hornton stone in our garden and when it is wet this becomes the colour of lead and the red streaks show up well. (Could these be the blood of the warriors who fell at the battle of Edgehill?) The Edgehill quarry is still working but those at Hornton have been closed for some years now. The Northamptonshire stone is a lovely ochre yellow, varying from village to village from tawny to gold. By the time you reach the panoramic views along the M62 in Yorkshire things have changed dramatically; the soil and stone of the treeless landscape are in almost mourning black. The drystone walls make a dark pattern defining the grass fields. The blackness of the stone of many buildings in the neighbouring towns is the unhappy result of years of smoke from the coal fires of these industrial areas. It has taken far too long for us to realise the importance of clean air — if we do now. Today the dreaded fall-out of industrial chemical waste is the problem. It makes me wonder how some of the most far-sighted founder members of the Royal Society would have reacted to our present-day problems. John Evelyn would certainly have been a strong influence among conservationists of wildlife, wildflowers and buildings, and a protector of our dignity of life. As far back as 1660 he was doing his best to protect the inhabitants of London from the black smoke caused by coal-burning. But Parliament and King were too occupied re-establishing a monarchical England to worry about such trivialities as the effects of smoke.

* * *     * * *     * * *

A visit to West Yorkshire would not be complete without going to Harlow Carr Gardens, the Wisley of the North. On this occasion I had the privilege of being taken round by the honorary director. It was a grey day but I found it all most inspiring. My first three choices were the vegetable and fruit plot, the immaculately kept display houses and (things never happen singly) the demonstration of the different stones that are suitable for making a rock garden. On each of the seven rock beds there were as yet no plants, only stones, just those that I had been thinking about on our journey. One had slabs of water-worn Yorkshire limestone, silvery-grey in contrast to the honey-coloured magnesium limestone quarried near Tadcaster from which York Minster was built. Another had soft tufa suitable for the embedding of small alpine plants which will thrive on it and make a neat carpet. Great slabs of greeny-blue Westmorland slate, shining and flat, which I associate with the fabulous rock gardens created for the Chelsea Flower Show, were used in another area. There was the Forest of Dean limestone, much pinker than any of the others, and the local millstone grit from Ilkley Moor, rather grey and forbidding. The Northamptonshire stone looked a deep, rich, browny-yellow, pristine in its unweathered state, as indeed were all the others, and I shall be interested to see the growth of lichen and moss in a year or two. It is an original and useful demonstration for anyone intending to create a rock garden; my decision was that one's own local stone, if available, is inevitably the best choice. Of course you should not rule out the possibility of using cement 'stones'; the colour used at the Harlow Car demonstration is very good but the truth about their identity is given away by the uniformity of their shapes.

※ ※ ※        ※ ※ ※        ※ ※ ※

Some people thrive best living in a community in close association with others, playing, as it were, a part in an orchestra or as a member of a team. Others are soloists and shine that way, though most of us live a family life. The pattern is followed through in nature, too, with birds and animals. Many species change their habits according to the season; often solitary or living in pairs in spring and summer, they form flocks before setting out on their migratory journeys. Our swallows have gone but the red-wings and fieldfares, both related to the thrushes, are common winter visitors. They are easy to recognise as they swirl in loose flocks across country lanes, often landing on the hedgerows to eat the hawthorn and other berries. Watch them and you will see them take off into the fields to find grubs and worms. They will stay in their flocks until breeding time comes round and they have moved north. Our resident starlings are always rather gregarious but at this time of the year they will gather in thousands. I sometimes wonder how the highest branches of our lime trees can bear their weight. I do not usually like their habits but I do appreciate them when they descend on my lawn and remove the wireworms; better still when they do this in neighbouring fields, where the wireworms devour the roots of grain and do much damage. The starlings then are welcome in large numbers, though their noise can be deafening. The finches form flocks in autumn and a charm of goldfinches feeding on a patch of thistles is a lovely sight. You will see groups of pied wagtails, up to about 20 of them in fields that are being worked. They are among the most attractive garden inhabitants in spring and summer but by this time of the year they are roosting in numbers. The majority of birds have individual nesting sites except of course those noisy rooks and many of the seabirds. Plovers living in pairs in summer will form flocks in autumn and winter. Partridges stay in their coveys until Christmas and then split into pairs in preparation for the breeding season. Many birds keep strictly to their territory in summer, especially our robins and wrens, but even the wrens will form groups in winter and cluster together to keep warm as they roost. Once you start considering these behaviour patterns you can draw parallels with human beings; some are social, some are not. What lesson we learn from this I am not sure.

      * * *      * * *      * * *

Wonderful spiders' webs have been festooning our garden recently. On misty mornings each gossamer thread has a spangle of moisture to outline its pattern. This morning they were almost the best I had ever seen. One thread was slung across a path to alight on top of a juniper. There was a perfect symmetrical web but the thread went on to the next plant, a grindelia given me several years ago by Tony Venison. Here each stem end had a veil of web over it and so, miraculously, it went on. To see the spider in action it is best to go out at night with a torch. The spider is carnivorous and gets rid of many of our garden pests for us. Most garden spiders probably remake their webs every day. I wonder if there is a connection between this proliferation of webs and the plagues of flies that infest old houses on sunny October days?

# NOVEMBER

The problem of where to store our apples is now a perennial one, for the stables and hay and apple lofts were converted 35 years ago into a retirement house for my father and mother-in-law; now this same building is my own home. Time and generations move swiftly on. When we came to live at Barnsley House, there were three large and prolific cooking-apple trees in the garden, all of different varieties and keeping qualities. They lasted the winter through. The ritual of picking and storing went on for days, supervised by my father-in-law using child labour — our sons. Everyone enjoyed it, with much friendly calling of instructions — "Can't you see that large red one by your right hand?" — and to-ing and fro-ing of large log baskets filled to the brim and taken gently on wheelbarrows. Picking was always more exciting than storing, which after a while became tedious. One full apple tray was stacked upon another, leaving enough space between each fruit for air circulation around the ripening apples. With careful management they lasted well into March, and throughout the winter stewed apples or huge baked ones were a regular part of our daily fare. On Sundays it would be something more exotic: Apple Betty, crumble, pie or dumplings. Then two of the old apple trees died, one from old age and the other from honey fungus. The third was hard pruned and in spite of its age still bears quantities of pale yellow fruit of a quality hard to beat; when baked they become lighter and more feathery than any soufflé. We planted new apple trees to replace the old, some as potential standards with spreading heads, others as neatly trained affairs growing on dwarf stock. There is a Bramley and a Charles Ross, two Cox's, three Sunsets and two Tydeman's Late Orange. Who, I wondered, as I laid them gently on a tray, was Tydeman or Charles Ross? As the trees grow so does the harvest and this year we have had a bumper crop which we have thoroughly enjoyed picking and storing. All the Laxton's Fortune were eaten in October and even earlier, their juiciness enjoyed by all. The Cox's are awaiting their ripening later. The huge Bramleys and Charles Ross will be eaten after Christmas. Each apple has been laid carefully on slatted trays in a spare bedroom, the floor surrounding them alive with mousetraps. A heavy pungent aroma hangs about the room while the apples are giving off their gases. In 1618 William Lawson's advice was as relevant as it is today. "For keeping, lay them in a dry loft, on heaps, ten or fourteen days, that they may sweat. Then dry them with a soft and cleane cloath and lay them thin abroad. Long keeping fruit would be turned once a month softly."

❖ ❖ ❖     ❖ ❖ ❖     ❖ ❖ ❖

Why do people spend so much time and energy with the leaf-sweeper? Here we don't make bonfires with the

as well as being a means of taking exercise. The object of pre-Christmas walks can be to keep an eye open for suitable Christmas decorations, some for the house and some for the church. We have a wonderful lane which has been walked and ridden for 2,000 years and so is haunted by ghosts of the past and full of good things in its hedges. Luckily no monster hedging-machine has yet been that way to spoil the growth of blackberries, wild roses, old man's beard and hazel nuts. Traditionally the evergreens for Christmas are holly and ivy to provide red and black berries, and mistletoe with its white translucent berries. These also bring good fortune and protection in the coming year. Mistletoe, or Kiss-and-Go, grown on apple and poplar trees, is the best for good luck. In Herefordshire a hundred years ago one third of all the apple trees had mistletoe growing on them. Each New Year's Eve a bough was picked and hung indoors as the clock struck twelve, the piece from the previous year being taken down and burnt. In nearby Worcestershire the chosen mistletoe branch was decked with nuts and ripe apples, tied with a ribbon and hung in the middle of the room. The just-marrieds would kiss under it and pick a berry, and then they would be blessed with a baby before next Christmas.

❉ ❉ ❉        ❉ ❉ ❉        ❉ ❉ ❉

Keeping a diary seems to run in my husband's family. His mother and grandfather both kept one for a long span of years and he himself has kept a diary without a break since he went to Eton in 1926. Between the three generations the diaries cover well over 100 years. They are a wonderful record and as I read them people and places long since forgotten flash through my memory and events are recaptured with varying vividness. I feel full of remorse that I have not mastered the art of spending even five minutes each evening recording the day's happenings. I have made several short-lived attempts, sometimes as a New Year resolution, as a genuine desire to keep a record of what was going on in the garden and the countryside. I have recently been admonished for my idleness and in consequence my new diary is a full four weeks old. It has the usual factual evidence of events; visitors, jelly-making from the quince crop, the mowing machine breaking down, the greenhouse roof collapsing and the glow of this autumn's leaves. In my attempt to make the diary of some practical help I would like to discover whether our vegetable and fruit growing efforts are an economy or an elaborately planned and time-consuming extravagance. Being a countrywoman I take it for granted that a vegetable patch is essential. Its success or failure depends on efficient planning but is it uneconomical? I do not believe it is but some people as they walk round my garden comment that each cabbage must cost a fortune. Only my full year's records will tell. I shall have to be scrupulous and include the cost of every item, from seeds and sprays to the time spent digging, weeding and harvesting. It will be even more difficult to assess the pleasures, such as those wonderful autumn raspberries, the variety called September, or the earliest of early potatoes, or the salads freshly picked and garnished with herbs.

❋ ❋ ❋        ❋ ❋ ❋        ❋ ❋ ❋

It is interesting to consider the challenges that were encountered recently when one of Gertrude Jekyll's border designs was faithfully re-planted. Combend at Elkstone in Gloucestershire is an old manor house on to which Asa Lingard, patron of the arts, incorporated a barn, making a house large enough for his collection of pictures and furniture. In 1929 he commissioned Gertrude Jekyll to make a planting plan for a 120 ft. by 8 ft. border, facing due south and backed by a 5 ft. Cotswold stone wall. Later this was dug up and the area put down to grass. In 1981 the present owners, Mr and Mrs Noel Gibbs, decided to restore it; planting started the following spring. The first problem, locating the plans, was easily overcome, for all Miss Jekyll's plans are on microfilm, held by the Garden History Society, to which they were generously donated by Berkeley University, California. Understanding the plans was another matter—Gertrude's handwriting is often difficult to decipher. Fortunately Tim Rees, a former student at Kew, is in charge of the work. With his flashes of intuition combined with Tony Lord's (of the National Trust) encyclopaedic knowledge of plants, most of the questions were solved. The border is a mixture of annuals and perennials, but some of Miss Jekyll's selected annual cultivars, such as snapdragons, are non-existent today. On occasions, only a colour description is given and this had to be accurately matched up. Personal choice inevitably begins to play a part and the restoration becomes a compromise between this, what is available and Miss Jekyll's intention. Tim Rees is clear on certain points; the emphasis here is predominantly on colour and the result is an excellent example of how Miss Jekyll used this in large drifts. There must be few of her borders restored so accurately which incorporate such precision over her use of annuals. Some people may wonder how Berkeley came to have the plans. The answer is straight-forward. During the war they were sold to raise money for the war effort and were bought by Beatrix Farrand, a great admirer of Gertrude Jekyll's work and a garden designer of special merit, well known for her work at Dumbarton Oaks. They became part of her library at Reef Point Gardens, at Bar Harbor in Maine. Her husband was a director of the Huntington Library at Los Angeles and when he died and Beatrix gave up her garden in Maine she donated her library to the University of California at Berkeley, for the Department of Landscape Architecture.

# DECEMBER

I love to receive a bunch of flowers. Who does not? And when the bunch is small enough to sit on my dressing table so that I wake in the morning with its clear scent in my room, it is a double bonus. We were puzzled by this bunch, though. Were they wild violets or cultivated Parma violets? They seemed to be a cross between the two, but in any case, why were they in full flower now, in early December, when they should be quiescent, waiting in the woods for springtime? I have them before me with their deep purple flowers drooping over the rim of their small container. They are not as large as the Parma violets I once grew in a frame but they are in every way as sweetly scented and the question is, how had they arrived in the wood beside my friends' house? Several years ago my friends had transplanted patches of wild violets to grow under their beech trees and had watched the patches grow wider and wider, making drifts of purple. Could they possibly be a cross between the wildlings and their superior Parma relations? We remembered how Parma violets had once been grown in frames in the walled garden of the neighbouring park. The garden boy picked and bunched buttonholes for the ladies to wear in the lapels of their elegant side-saddle coats on hunting days. All through history violets have held a special place for their scent, their use and romance. The Greeks picked them for garlands and chaplets; the Romans made violet wine and fried them with slices of orange and lemon; the romantic poet Fortunas, Bishop of Poitiers, sent gifts of violets to St. Radegunde as decoration for her church. Perhaps best of all, the beautiful Empress Josephine embroidered her wedding dress with violets, after which they were a signature of love between her and Napoleon. No other flower so small has been held in such high esteem as *Viola odorata.*

\* \* \*    \* \* \*    \* \* \*

At this time of the year when hedges are bare it is fascinating to see how each field of winter corn has been drilled. I asked my farmer son why, on the best of farms, there are lines like tramlines where the drill has plainly missed two rows. He described how the drilling pattern will govern the method of covering the ground in subsequent operations, fertiliser spreading, spraying and harvesting. During the work the tractor wheels could well knock down a considerable quantity of corn so the tramlines are left at regular intervals, the spacing appropriate to the width of the spray and fertiliser spreader. When the field is square and flat there is no problem, for the drill will go round the field twice or thrice, then set off on a regular up and down pattern, remembering to leave the tramlines. But when the field is an awkward shape the subtlety of the operation becomes apparent;

curves in the boundary are ignored and the resulting un-
prepared ground is infilled later. It is noticeable that a
field on a bank has its lines going straight up and down
the incline—the safest way to drive a combine. Time is
an all-important factor—farmers have to make the most
of dry days—so the question of how the tractor or combine will turn at each corner can make a considerable
difference to the acreage covered. Without careful planning as much as 20 per cent of working time could be
spent 'out of work' while the tractors or combines turn.
It is much the same principle with a lawnmower. Husbandry has for centuries been concerned with the same
problems as beset the 20th century farmer. Seven hundred
years ago Walter of Henley referred to the farmer standing
at "the landes ende and looking towards the other ende;
and then ye may see howe the corne groweth."

                      ℒ ℒ ℒ           ℒ ℒ ℒ           ℒ ℒ ℒ

Recently I have been in a garden in Northamptonshire
where the owner is planting two scented borders. The
site is marvellous as the two parallel, long, inward-sloping
beds are divided by a grass path where I hope the scents
will hang upon the air. It should be a lovely calm, wind-
less pocket. The garden is open to the public from Easter
until autumn so we have not used any winter flowers or
shrubs, with the wealth of fragrance these can provide.
Often you hear people say they have a poor sense of smell.
Is it really poor, I wonder, or have they never bothered

or learnt to enjoy the scents around them? Now is the time to experiment. The next three months are rich in garden scents. Some, like that of the winter honeysuckle, *Lonicera fragrantissima*, will hang upon the air, while there are others like winter-sweet, *Chimonanthus praecox*, whose flowers must be held in the hand or better still be brought indoors to give freely of their fragrance. Many of the Viburnum family have a wonderful scent — if you choose wisely you can have them in flower from late autumn right through until spring. Our *V. farreri* has been flowering since September. The witch hazels and azaras and the ambrosial scented daphnes are mostly winter flowering. Small plants such as *Viola odorata* and the winter iris, *I. unguicularis* (stylosa) with a fragrance of cowslips and honey, make lovely indoor scented posies. In March the early daffodils will be out and by then, if you have practised, perhaps your nose will have become accustomed to trying out and finding the best scents in the garden. Remember that some are only available as dusk descends, for these are the flowers, like *Daphne laureola*, which hold their fragrance until evening when the moths are about ready to pollinate the flowers.

\* \* \*　　　\* \* \*　　　\* \* \*

It always falls to my lot to do the church flowers in December. This dates back to the years when we grew chrysanthemums and always had plenty to fill the vases. Now the greenhouse space is occupied by scented-leaved

114

pelargoniums and a variety of other tender plants but no chrysanthemums. For the first Sunday in the month I had a lovely time wandering in the garden. Flowers were scarce; a few bedraggled roses, the last of the nerines and some fragrant *Viburnum bodnantense* were the only possibilities so instead I settled for decorative leaves. How satisfying this proved to be; sprays of grey eucalyptus to contrast with apple-green hart's tongue ferns, golden privet and golden lonicera, blending with holly "Silver Queen" and dark green ivies with variegated periwinkles. There are still plenty of berries about so I chose a selection of white, yellow and red sorbus. I am not adept at flower arranging but the sheer quality of the foliage and berries was exciting.

      *& & &*       *& & &*       *& & &*

Now the shortest days are on us and darkness descends soon after four o'clock. I can come in from the garden to the welcome of a warm fire and the prospect of a long peaceful evening spent with all those books which have been accumulating on my table. Some have inspired me to use more herbs in the kitchen or to experiment with old ideas like using saponaria leaves and roots as a gentle soap to revitalise old and faded fabrics. A satisfying occupation when hard frosts make outdoor activities unattractive, but you must have a supply of roots ready dug and handy. Soapwort reminds me of a hot day in Ethiopia when we came upon a large patch of it growing beside a lake, and sure enough this was where the women did their laundry.

* * *     * * *     * * *

This New Year's Eve as the clock strikes midnight the '80s start. A quick glance back over the past ten years and country people will remember the great drought, the great frost, the hue and cry raised against hunting and coursing, the increased vogue for visiting historic country houses, their estates and gardens. What perhaps are less obvious to us are the increasingly grave threats to the plant kingdom, with over 25,000 flowering plant species believed to be in danger. A Red Data Book compiled at Kew and published in 1978 by the International Union for Conservation of Nature and Natural Resources gives detailed case histories of 250 threatened plants from a wide range of different habitats. One of our resolutions for the next ten years could be to become more positive in promoting conservation of our country surroundings. Leisure for town dwellers will mean extra time spent in the country so the countryside will inevitably get more wear and tear but let us hope it will be associated with an increase in awareness and respect and a decrease in vandalism. For as Moses Cook wrote over 300 years ago, "Those that are wasters and wilful spoilers of trees and plants, without just reason to do so, have seldom prospered in this world."

116